stitches, straps & layers

MAGGIE GREY

Contents

Introduction

With so many new materials coming on the market, we sometimes forget to consider the fabrics and art materials that we already have in our cupboards. This book aims to redress this balance and encourages the reader to look at new ways of combining fabric and stitch, enhanced by innovative techniques and embellishments.

REUSE & SAVE

Most of the materials will be found in your stash. Some will be recycled – tissue, cardboard and metal from purée tubes – so good for the environment and good for our purses, too. **Look for this sign for a money-saving idea.**

The book aims to build textiles from the bottom up – initially looking at backgrounds before applying further materials – to include slips built up from fabric, paper and mixed media. By working in layers, it is possible to achieve an effect that belies the simplicity of its structure. Finally, straps offer exciting ideas with a variety of uses. The sections of the book reflect this approach, being divided into backgrounds, applied elements of stitch, and strips and straps.

Of course, we shall be stretching this idea. In each section, a basic technique is examined in detail before exploring ideas for 'customising' and extending it. New techniques mix with old favourites and the layering process makes it easier to achieve a balanced design, as the elements can be placed and rearranged before the final application.

So raid the stash, bring out the 'stuff' and get layering.

'Celtic Pod' vessel. Straps made from silk carrier rods with couched threads were wrapped to form a vessel shape. Additional stitching was added using techniques from the book.

How the book works

Before we leap into the section on making backgrounds, let's be clear on the objectives. We're aiming to make textiles using a traditional basis of fabric and stitch, with the odd foray into paper and paint.

Whichever route you prefer (and I hope you will try both), the method will involve the use of a decorated base, similar to those shown here, on which will be built layers of stitched or constructed pieces. I like to call these slips or patches. Some of them are also shown in the photograph and range from cut-out pieces of stitching to fragments of paper displaying faded lettering. Metal, especially recycled material, adds a lustrous gleam when applied. Even the humble curtain ring can add dramatic emphasis when wrapped, beaded and suspended over a suitable bottom layer. Of course, you can always make the slip first and then construct a background for it. All things are possible.

Straps are made from strips of stitched or embellished material and can form an exciting component. Imagine the one shown opposite, laid over a rich background or wrapped around a shape for a vessel. It's also an easy matter to form these into belts or handbag straps. Joined together, they could form an airy background of their own – or even be used as a curtain.

Materials

You can use mostly what's in the cupboard but the following items will be useful:

- velvet, felt and some sheer fabrics

- Abaca paper (Tissutex)

- fusible webbing (Bondaweb) and foil

- yarns, beads, sequins and charms from the stash

- water-soluble film or fabric

- scrim or vanishing muslin (Thermogauze)

- metal from purée tubes and tissue paper from packaging.

Any additional materials will be explained as they are needed.

I do recommend investigating your local government's recycling initiatives. Our council has a superb facility called 'The Scrapstore' where you can fill a huge bag with goodies for next to nothing. On my last visit I found foil, Tyvek, scrim and a strange form of netting. Another time they may have nothing of interest but it's always worth a look.

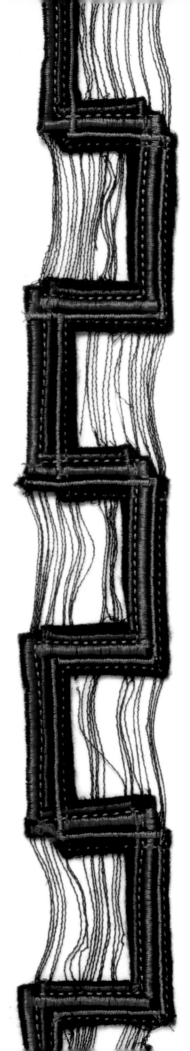

OPPOSITE: Some of the backgrounds and motifs that will be used to build up finished pieces.

RIGHT: A strap made by stitching satin stitch bands on felt. This was cut out and placed on water-soluble film for the lacy lengths of straight stitching.

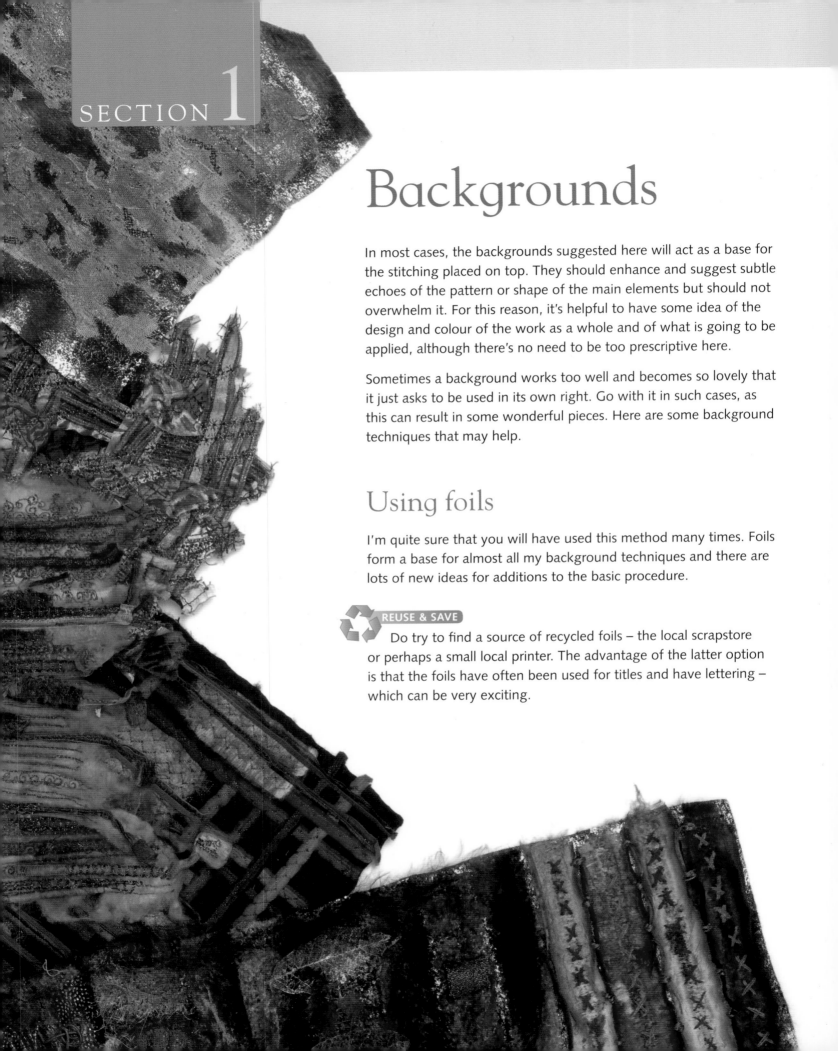

Backgrounds

In most cases, the backgrounds suggested here will act as a base for the stitching placed on top. They should enhance and suggest subtle echoes of the pattern or shape of the main elements but should not overwhelm it. For this reason, it's helpful to have some idea of the design and colour of the work as a whole and of what is going to be applied, although there's no need to be too prescriptive here.

Sometimes a background works too well and becomes so lovely that it just asks to be used in its own right. Go with it in such cases, as this can result in some wonderful pieces. Here are some background techniques that may help.

Using foils

I'm quite sure that you will have used this method many times. Foils form a base for almost all my background techniques and there are lots of new ideas for additions to the basic procedure.

REUSE & SAVE

Do try to find a source of recycled foils – the local scrapstore or perhaps a small local printer. The advantage of the latter option is that the foils have often been used for titles and have lettering – which can be very exciting.

I have a personal preference for plain gold foil, with just a hint of other colours. Silver is very 'in your face' and should be used sparingly. The foils used with dots are quite subtle and look good on velvet.
Here's the basic method:

1   Cut a piece of velvet or felt to the required size. Cut fusible webbing slightly smaller.

2   Iron the webbing to the fabric using a hot iron, making sure that it's well caught down.

3   Cool the iron to about the silk setting and lay a piece of gold foil (shiny side up) on top of the webbing. Cover with baking paper and then run the iron lightly over the gold.

4   Peel off the gold and repeat in another area. Repeat with other colours – sparingly. If you have ironed too heavily and overdone the foil, try using a heat tool to knock it back a little.

Make any additions – as suggested in the next section – before ironing chiffon, Lutradur or Abaca tissue paper over the top.

TOP: Fusible webbing is ironed onto velvet and the paper removed.
CENTRE: Gold and blue metallic foil were ironed onto this.
BOTTOM: Leaves were placed on the velvet before the webbing was applied. Foil was then added and black sheer fabric ironed over the top.

EXTENDING THE BASICS

This background is so versatile. All manner of threads, sequins, yarns and fibres can be trapped between the foil layer and the top fabric. Most flat items – sequins rather than beads, for example – will stick to the webbing, even though there is foil on top. They all benefit from stitch but, if you use a thin or stretchy velvet, always back with a stabiliser – Vilene or felt – to avoid puckers. Here are some ideas:

- Apply the webbing dots instead of ordinary webbing. These just hold the foil on the dot. Try working in bands or shapes, leaving spaces between. Use a different colour foil on each band, as you can see in Angie Hughes' stitched piece, shown here.

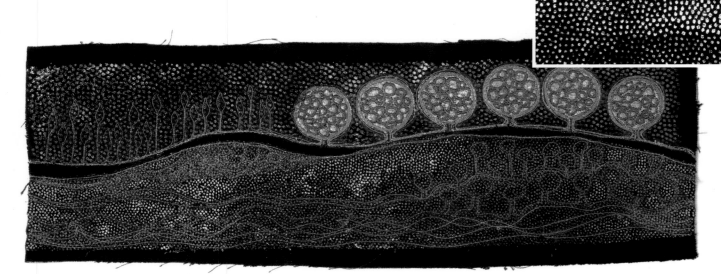

- Sprinkle some tiny sequins over the webbing and foil before ironing very sheer fabric on top. Abaca tissue is particularly good with this effect as the matt paper enhances the contrast of the shiny sequins. It is possible to stitch over the plastic ones, too.

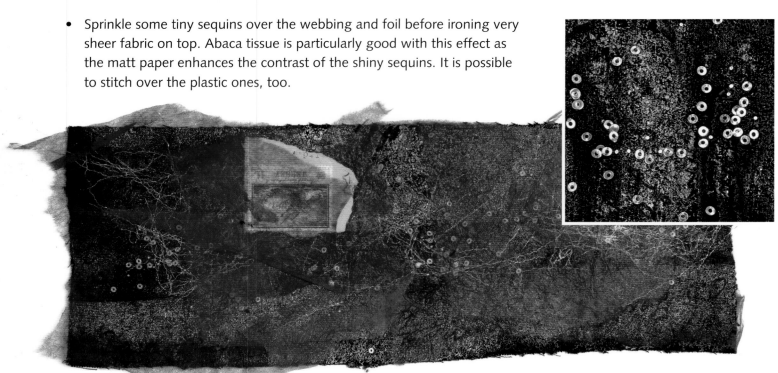

REUSE & SAVE

- Chop up some threads – a mix of glitzy and plain colour would be good. Save the cut ends when you are hand stitching, or the starting threads from metallics when machining. Sprinkle over the webbing. In a similar way, use some Angelina fibres – the metallic ones that don't fuse with heat are ideal. Iron chiffon, organza or fine Lutradur over the top. An exciting option is to stitch this surface and then use a heat tool to reveal the fibres.

- Look for figured velvets for the base layer – some have raised stripes, others random lines or patterns. The foil will only show on the raised areas. Corduroy and finer needlecords will also give good results. These fabrics work particularly well when a sheer is used on top and zapped with a heat tool, revealing the shapes below. Don't be a fabric snob – my best piece from this technique came from some horrid Crimplene-like fabric in the 'giving it away' bin at the local fabric shop.

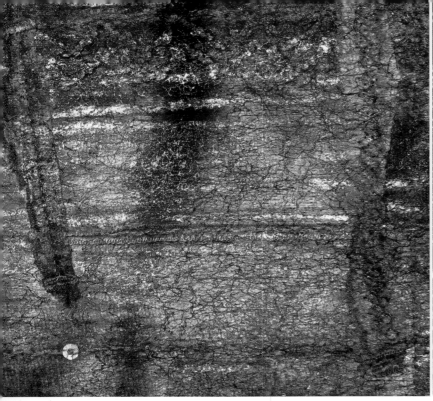

GOSSAMER FUSE

This is a very fine variety of fusible webbing. It doesn't hold so well for bonding fabrics but it's great for foiling and can be used instead of solid webbing. It gives a lighter coating of foil and, on smooth fabrics, an attractive broken effect. This webbing does not have a backing, so make sure you lay baking paper on top before ironing. Try painting the white version – it works with most paints. Allow to dry well before ironing onto fabric and foiling.

LEFT: Gossamer Fuse on velvet, some with trapped lace and threads.

OPPOSITE: Trapped leaves were partly torn away to reveal the velvet below. The foil had lettering which was used as text. Hand stitching techniques were added as a finishing touch.

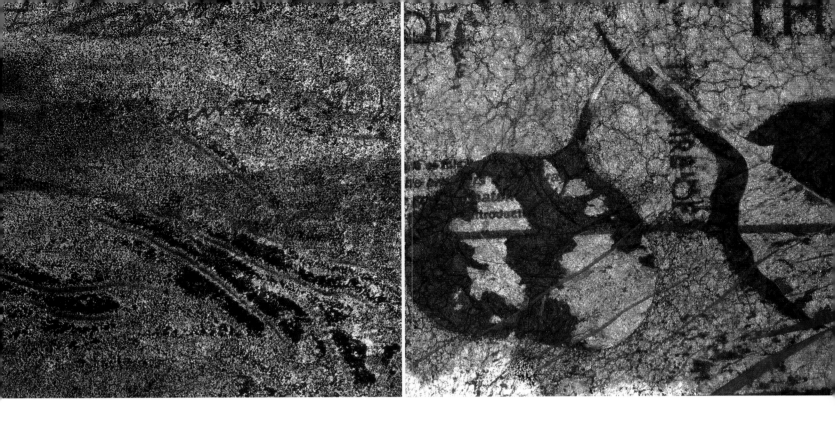

TRAPPING AND VOIDING

Lay some threads on the base fabric before ironing the webbing over the top. Then foil and remove the threads. Different thicknesses have very different effects.

Take this a stage further by trapping other shapes – perhaps cut out some paper hearts or geometric shapes. Leaves work well. You could use real leaves or skeleton leaves. There is also the option of placing the leaves on top of the foil and leaving them in place.

STITCH AND BURN-BACK TECHNIQUES

Iron on the foil and then allow a day or so for the stickiness to leave the webbing. Now stitch some random satin stitch blobs by using your widest zigzag stitch and closing the length so that the stitches are very close together. Leave the feed dogs up and gently pull the fabric from side to side as you stitch. If you have a pressure control for the foot, set it to the highest setting. When you have stitched the 'blob', lift the foot and pull to a new location, without cutting the thread and leaving it to show on top. Iron sheer fabrics or Lutradur over the top and zap to show stitching.

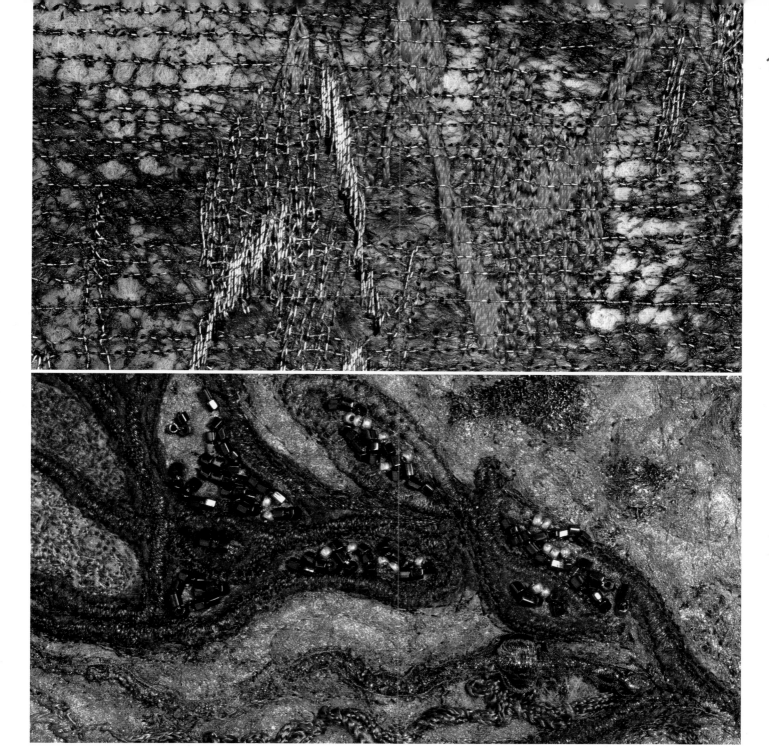

Alternatively, build up the foil in the usual way. Place medium-weight Lutradur over the top and stitch, using straight lines or random stitching. Don't make the stitching too heavy. Paint the Lutradur with 'runny' paint in a bright colour, making sure you select a 'safe to heat' paint. Zap and paint again with gold acrylic.

TOP: Blobs of stitching on Lutradur with the Lutradur zapped after stitching.

ABOVE: Cut-out felt outlines filled with beads were stitched onto Lutradur. The piece was painted with gold paint after zapping.

Printed and stamped bases

Another useful base material for the layered approach is printed or stamped fabric. At its simplest, this could just be a piece of plain, smooth fabric with motifs stamped onto it using a fairly large foam or rubber stamp. This could be stitched in straight lines or have pintucks worked over it to distort the motifs (see page 36 for pintuck techniques).

It is even more satisfying to make the stamps yourself. You can buy easy-carve rubber blocks and cut motifs or texture with a lino-cutting tool. If you are working to a theme, this will obviously provide a better way of working to your design theme. Think about the positive and negative areas of the design and draw it onto the block, shading in the parts that will be cut away. Also remember that the design will be reversed. This is important for lettering, so scan it into the computer and flip – or trace it off and reverse the drawing.

BELOW: Stamped and stitched pieces, one with pintucks.

REUSE & SAVE

A good cheap printing block can be made from a polystyrene meat or vegetable tray from the supermarket. I like to use this with acrylic paints. Work like this:

1 Cut the edges from the tray so that you have a flat surface. Lay the design, reversed if necessary, over the polystyrene and draw through the paper, pressing hard to transfer the design lines. This will probably destroy the design, so use a copy. Make a handle from parcel tape and glue it on the back of the block.

2 Prepare the fabric, ironing out wrinkles if necessary. Lay it on a 'cushion' of kitchen paper.

3 Roll out paint quite thinly on a piece of glass or plastic (or a thick polythene sheet). Too little is better than too much which may clog the lines of the print. Use no more than three colours or it will be muddy.

4 Lay the block on the paint and press gently, then print a couple of times on scrap paper. This gets the print working and gives you an idea of how the paint should be rolled.

5 When you are happy with the result, print on the fabric. Renew the paint and re-roll as necessary.

The blocks can be printed next to each other for an all-over design or spaced in a random fashion.

These backgrounds look good with a little foil applied. To keep a light touch, tear strips of the Bondaweb (fusible webbing) and lay over the printed background. Lay baking paper over the top and iron with a hot iron. Foil as before.

Misty Fuse webbing is also good here and can be laid all over the surface – no need for strips. Use a stabiliser before stitching these backgrounds.

Consider stitching some sheer fabric over the top. This could be left as it is or burned back with a heat tool.

BELOW: This simple linear design (from a pizza base) was printed on white cotton which was then dabbed with teabags. Cast paper and scrim decorated the central area with stitched straps forming borders.

Paper for backgrounds

There are lots of reasons for using paper as a background and it is not as fragile as you may think, especially if it is acrylic waxed. Another good reason is that tissue paper is often free and the tissue that comes with shoes, for instance, is thicker than the stuff you buy in packets.

A drawback of paper is that it can be difficult to stitch but, if we follow the basic felt, tissue, foil routine, this should not be a problem. The embellisher machine works well when used on paper and is good for integrating strips of paper into a background.

Crumple the tissue very lightly and then lay it on the foiled felt, covering with baking paper and ironing very well with a hot iron.

Let loose the imagination with the painting and use some of the wonderful new paints such as Starburst Stains. One or two colours won't break the budget and will last for ages.

A variety of painted papers are shown here. Some are stencilled, some painted with walnut ink and some lightly sprayed with gold metallic sprays. One of the pieces has been decorated with straight lines of stitching.

PAINT EFFECTS

Another joy of paper is the ability to use those techniques that just don't work on fabric, such as ink and bleach, and stamping with embossing powder or encaustic wax. Stencils and stamps are, of course, brilliant on paper and the polystyrene blocks also work well on paper.

Try using black tissue paper or painting with black ink. When dry, spray with Moon Shadow Mist and, while this is wet, spray again with Glitz Spritz. You'll find more details of these paints and inks in the free glossary on the d4daisy website www.d4daisy.com.

STITCHING

Paper benefits from stitching, both to strengthen it and to integrate any 'over-the-top' paint effects. I find that the most effective stitching is simple straight lines that do not overpower anything placed on the top. If a stencil has been used, this could be accented with free machine stitching or the stencil design could be repeated in a plain area.

TOP: Detail from 'Celtic Spear' (see page 92) showing the stencilled paper background and the stitched bands of painted paper.
LEFT: The stitched paper seen on page 19 has been used as a background for a cast paper face with carrier rod straps acting as borders.

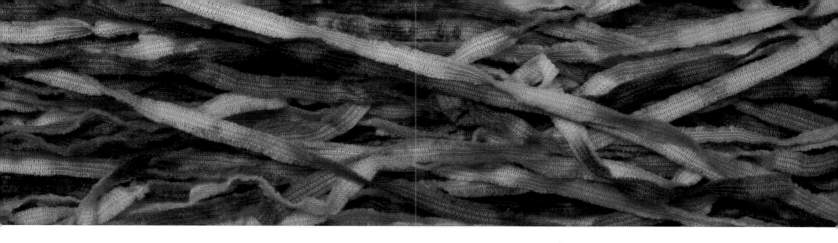

Working up the base

Now we can start building on the foiled base. In this section, we'll be looking at techniques for applying fragments and distressed fabrics, stitching, stripped carrier rods and fancy yarns over the foil to add interest.

APPLIED YARNS

A huge variety of ribbons and yarns are available and the ones that I find most useful are the soft, flat woollen tapes (Tagliatelli) made by Colinette. But do try others, especially those in the remainder bin at the knitting shop. Even the ones that may look quite unlikely can sometimes produce great results.

The tapes can be stitched directly to the background and, if you are using foiled velvet, this can be allowed to show in places. If the yarns are to cover the entire ground, work on a good-tempered fabric such as felt or stabilised cotton. As the pieces we are making here are destined to be backgrounds, the stitching is best kept plain. Straight stitch with the feed dogs up gives a good result. Utility stitches will also work and will provide added interest without taking over the piece. Think about colour schemes and consider the top thread, using one that will complement or contrast with the yarns used.

When stitching consider
the following:

- Either secure one strip of
  yarn at a time or spray the
  fabric with temporary adhesive
  and lay on all the yarns
  before stitching.

- Combine a variety of yarns,
  ribbons, metallic cords and
  strips of purée tube metal.

- For difficult yarns of the frayed
  or hairy type, lay on the
  background and cover with
  water-soluble film. Place in a
  frame and stitch – a metallic
  thread could look good.
  When stitched, dissolve the
  film. Free machining could be
  used to good effect here.

- Plait or weave the flat tape,
  keeping the yarn flat as you
  work. Pin or tack the woven
  strips onto a piece of water-
  soluble fabric or film, keeping
  them close to each other.
  Free machine them together,
  meandering along the lines of
  the weaving and making sure
  they are firmly attached to
  each other. Dissolve the film
  when stitching is complete.
  This gives a soft, loose-woven
  fabric that can be stretched
  over a foiled background.

RIGHT: A variety of backgrounds made
from couched yarns.

ABOVE: Cable stitch worked using jap gold on the bobbin and contrasting threads on the top. A sample by Val Campbell-Harding.

BELOW: Wrapped straws with small squares of water-soluble stitching.

 REUSE & SAVE

- Work cable stitch in geometric patterns. Wind a chunky thread onto the bobbin and work upside down. Mark the pattern, if you are using one, on interfacing and iron this to the reverse of the work. Think beyond the usual perlé threads and consider using some of the metal threads used for goldwork, such as jap gold. Look out for cheap Christmas cords which can look wonderful used in the bobbin. The thread on the top should couch the bobbin thread, so take the colour into account.

- Wrap some straws (save them from take-away drinks – some of these are a very sexy black) with the tapes and couch them to backgrounds.

Distressed fabrics

Building up a layer of frayed and tatty fabric on a foiled ground can look great and brings to mind historic sources such as faded and fraying treasures, old embroidered books, bags or garments. There are several ways to do this.

This little sweetie bag is based on an Elizabethan pea motif. It is made with a foiled velvet background built up with Thermogauze and scrim to give an impression of distressed fabric. The little pea pod tassels are made from felt with tiny pearls.

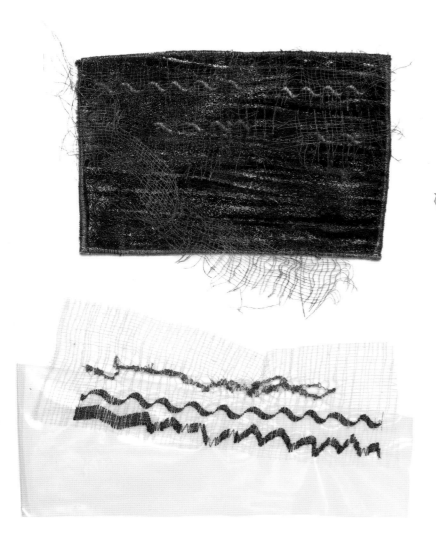

SCRIM

REUSE & SAVE

There is a huge international debate over this fabric – check the d4daisy website (www.d4daisy.com) glossary for photos to see exactly what it is and read the definition. For our purposes, scrim is an inexpensive fabric with a very loose weave. In the UK this can sometimes be purchased, very cheaply, as 'builders' scrim'.

1   Paint the scrim (any paint is fine) before applying to a background and allow it to dry.

2   Lay over the background and stitch very lightly. Use a pattern stitch or bursts of satin stitch – thin stitching will lose definition.

3   Take a pair of sharp scissors and pull out thread from the scrim, leaving the stitches and some of the fragmented fabric.

ABOVE: Scrim, laid on a foiled velvet background and stitched with pulled zigzags and automatic patterns. It is also possible to stitch on the scrim first and then apply it to the background.

BELOW: A lovely fragmented effect is created when vanishing muslin is stamped with gold paint and then distressed with a heat tool. This is fragile but it could be stitched before painting to give greater strength.

VANISHING MUSLIN (THERMOGAUZE)

Another useful material to apply to a background, especially when a distressed look is needed, is a heat-activated fabric called vanishing muslin (Thermogauze). The piece below was stamped with gold paint before zapping.

This muslin-like material can be stitched and then heated with a heat tool or iron to remove or shred the fabric. It can be painted but this may cause smoking, so either paint after using the heat tool or work outside. Work like this:

1 Lay the vanishing muslin (Thermogauze) over a foiled velvet background. If you don't want to cover the entire area, just cut pieces and lay them over the velvet.

2 Now stitch – freely or with the foot on, as you prefer – over the vanishing muslin (Thermogauze), securing it to the background. If working to a design, consider related motifs as these can look great when frayed. Use stitches as marks but don't stitch too heavily all over.

Two backgrounds have been given the vanishing muslin treatment. One has been edged with carrier rods (see page 30) and decorated with wrapped pipe-cleaners. They now need further layers to complete them.

3   Working in a well-ventilated
    room, use the heat tool
    over the vanishing muslin
    (Thermogauze). It will go
    brown and can be rubbed or
    brushed away. Don't overheat
    or you'll have none left.

4   Damp lightly and spray with
    colour, avoiding the base
    velvet as much as possible –
    cover with paper as a mask.

Very light stitching is all that is needed to
produce delicate motifs such as these fantasy
plants. They could be applied to a background
by hand to preserve their delicacy. Stitching
them by machine would flatten them.

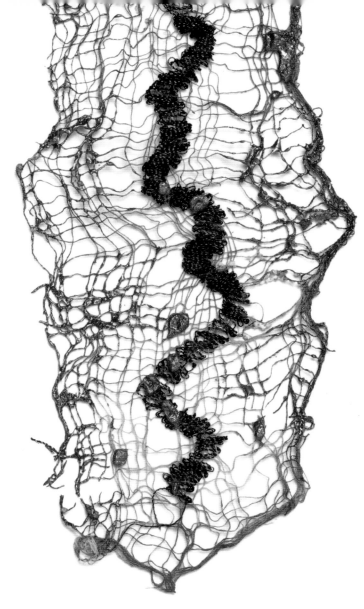

EMBOSSING POWDER

An interesting effect can be achieved with embossing powder on stitched Thermogauze or open-weave scrim (use pulled satin stitch and lay the scrim on water-soluble paper). Dissolve the water-soluble paper and paint with acrylic paint. Then sprinkle on the embossing powder. Shake off the remainder of the powder and heat carefully – keep the heat tool high as the fabric can singe.

Apply to a background by hand.

Two samples showing the effect of a very light coat of embossing powder. The one above is worked on 'builder's scrim' and the other is stamped on vanishing muslin.

Carrier rods

These are the compacted waste fibres from the silk-spinning process which get wrapped around the rods until they build up and are cut free. They make great backgrounds, either on the foiled velvet or on plain felt. You can buy them undyed or ready to use, having been dyed in luscious colours like the ones shown here.

Use them as they are to edge small pieces of work. Just roll them over the edge and hand stitch to the back of the textile – no need to stitch the front. You can see this effect on page 26.

Carrier rods can be purchased already dyed in wonderful colours.

REUSE & SAVE

The really good thing about them is that they can be separated into layers, giving you a lot more for your money. I find the best way to separate the layers is to roll up the short side, first one way and then the other. Then rub them between your fingers until the edges show some separation and you can peel them apart. If you want to keep them in rod shapes, you will get two or three but you could go on to four or five for shorter strips.

ABOVE: The rods can be split into layers to make them go further.

This piece by Janet Crowther is a delightful collage of separated carrier rods and flat knitting tape. It is enhanced by pintucks and machine patterns.

STITCHING TO A BACKGROUND

For a simple but effective background, just lay the rods on foiled velvet – allowing a little of the background to show – and then stitch each rod down. The stitching is effective with a pattern, if you have one, but straight lines of stitch look good, too. For a bigger background, work in rows.

Try the following to extend the technique:

- Combine with couched yarns or metal threads.

- Cut up the rods and arrange in geometric patterns on the background.

- Work on unfoiled velvet or plain dark felt.

- Stitch larger satin stitch patterns over the top. Try 'pulled' zigzags, slightly curved.

USING THE CARRIER RODS

The stitched rods can be made up into brilliant backgrounds or can be used just as they are for vessels, book covers or bags.

ABOVE: Anna Nowicki's delightful little bags also use carrier rods and flat knitting tapes. The colours are carefully chosen to tone or contrast. A little machine patterning adds detail.

OPPOSITE: Separated rods and knitting tapes are stitched to black felt, using simple straight stitching. Narrow curves of satin stitch are worked over the top. These can be stitched by gently pulling at the work as the short lines are stitched. *(Val Campbell-Harding)*

Making backgrounds with the embellisher machine

If you own an embellisher, try using any of the methods discussed, adapting the method to suit the machine. Here are some ideas:

1 Machine stitch some silk rods and then apply with the embellisher. Some of the stitching will be destroyed and this gives an interesting effect. Try hand stitching them too – and then embellishing.

2 Use a fabulous ribbon – the silk velvet ones from Mulberry Silks are wonderful. Embellish each side, leaving the centre untouched to preserve the gleam.

3

Foil the background, lay
skeleton leaves on top,
cover with sheer fabric and
embellish all around the
leaves without touching
them. Then, very lightly,
embellish into the leaf.
Take care not to destroy
too much of it.

4

Stitch a foiled velvet
surface with satin stitch
blobs. Embellish painted
Lutradur on top and use a
heat tool to burn back to
the stitches.

5

Use stitched or puffed
scrim and embellish, using
a sheer fabric to apply the
scrim to the background
if necessary.

6

Try painted tissue paper
and paint with acrylic
wax after embellishing to
strengthen the surface.
The piece is finished with
a beaded tassel.

Pintucks

Victorians loved tucks on mourning dress, nice and wide to show their grief – and their wealth. Proper pintucks, tucks that are the width of a pin, bring to mind crisp white nighties. Pintucks can enhance a fabric in their own right and can be manipulated, cut up and shaped to form bags, garments etc. They also make great backgrounds. My friend Janet Crowther has done some really exciting work with pintucks so I've persuaded her to write about her techniques. You'll find examples of her work throughout the book.

Layers of sheer fabrics look wonderful when enhanced by swirls of pintucks. This sample could be laid over velvet for a bag or used just as it is for wearable art. *(Janet Crowther)*

HOW TO PINTUCK

Hand-stitched pintucks are made by folding the fabric along the grain and stitching the two layers together, a pin's width from the fold, to make a tuck. That is one way with a sewing machine. A quicker way is to use a twin needle and a pintuck presser foot on your machine. Twin needles come in sizes from 1.6 mm for skinny pintucks to 6 mm for big, fat, and perhaps corded, pintucks.

Depending on the make of your machine, one pintuck foot may 'fit all', or you may have to buy a pintuck presser foot to fit the twin needle size. It is possible not to use a pintuck foot. A standard foot will work, particularly if you do not wish to stitch neat parallel rows of tucks.

Work like this for a twin-needled pintuck:

1   Using two reels of thread (thread can be reeled onto a spare bobbin to use as the second thread), thread your machine as normal, taking care not to cross the threads around each other. If the tension disc is visible, place a thread to each side of it.

2   Tighten the top tension a little and tighten the bottom tension by turning the little screw on the bobbin holder clockwise. Start with a quarter turn (there is the saying 'righty tighty, lefty loosy' to help you remember). Make a note of the angle of the screw head before you change it and don't forget to return it to normal after pintucking.

3   Thread the bobbin in the usual manner. Some machines have a setting for twin-needle stitching, so consult your manual.

4   Set your machine to straight stitch, feed dog up. The bobbin thread will zigzag between the two top threads. This pulls the fabric together and creates the pintuck.

Experiment with your tension and stitch size until you have the tuck you desire. Some makes of machine are better at pintucks than others. Remember that pintucks use fabric at a great rate, so allow plenty before you start.

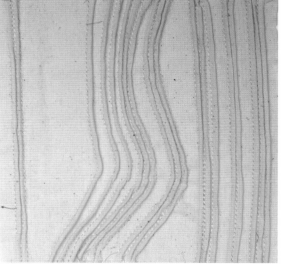

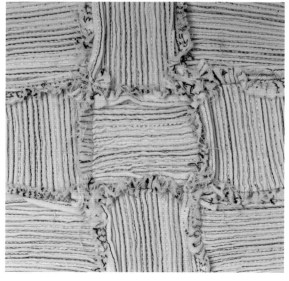

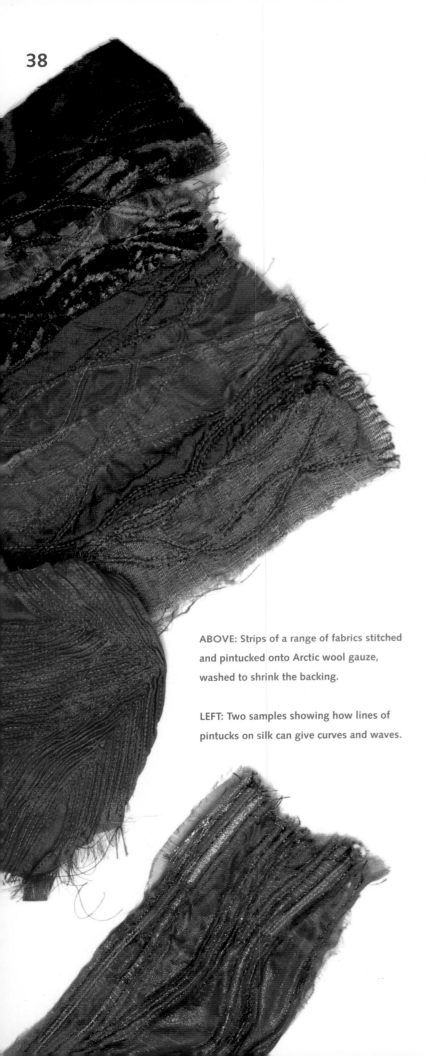

ABOVE: Strips of a range of fabrics stitched and pintucked onto Arctic wool gauze, washed to shrink the backing.

LEFT: Two samples showing how lines of pintucks on silk can give curves and waves.

TAKING IT FURTHER

Here Janet Crowther gives some ideas to try for creating pintuck backgrounds:

- Pintucks do not have to run with the grain of the fabric. Try on the bias, in curves and waves.

- Use the same thread on top and bottom for nice neat pintucks or try two different threads on the top and yet another on the bobbin. The bobbin thread will show through if you stitch on a sheer fabric. Metallic threads add a bit of glitz.

- Make corded pintucks. As you stitch your pintuck, feed a cord under your fabric between the twin needles so that it is enclosed by the stitching. Coloured wire can be used instead of cord and then the piece can be manipulated. Use sheer fabrics and coloured cords.

- Use layers of fabrics and cut through the pintucks in places to reveal the cord or wire.

- Try vanishing muslin (Thermogauze) or kunin felt and burn holes in them with a heat tool.

- Stitch pintucks over pintucks.

- Add other stitches such as vermicelli or granite stitch.

- Stitch pintucks in rows cut into strips and weave the strips together. Stab stitch by hand on the top to secure.

- Use automatic patterns on ticking fabric and then pintuck down the lines or across the lines.

- Stitch across pintucks at intervals so that they lie in one direction. Turn and stitch the other way so that they lie in the opposite direction.

- Use pintucks for shaping, creating textured lumps and bumps.

LEFT: Layers of sheers pintucked over cords, cut through in places to reveal cords.

ABOVE: Bits and pieces of fabrics stitched
together, then pintucked and cut into strips.
The strips were woven together and restitched.

BELOW: Multiple layers give an intricate surface.
Here the bottom layer has areas stitched using
vermicelli and granite stitch, the next
layer is pintucks over pintucks and the
top layer uses vermicelli stitch over
sheers, pintucked and burnt back.

A sample of dense free machining had failed in its
intended purpose as the design was lost in the colours.
This didn't matter at all when it became the background
for a bag. It was given a focal point with the addition of
stitched felt motifs.

The failed experiments box

This is the name given by one of my friends to the other form of stash that we all have – the unfinished work, the disasters, the samples from classes or trials that didn't quite work. Any of these may be suitable for turning into a background, so go and have a look. Here are some ideas:

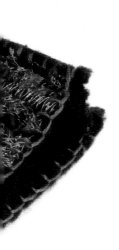

- Iron foil over the top of dyeing disasters – try using Misty Fuse webbing, or Bondaweb with Markal Paintstik over the top.

- Stamp with puff paint.

- Add more stitch to failed machine embroidery experiments – the bag shown left is an example of this.

- Paint pale, boring pieces with bright-coloured acrylics to change the texture and the colour.

- Piece together oddments and add paint to bring them all together.

I'm sure you'll think of lots more that can be done if you have a play with all the bits in your box – layer them up, pull them apart … be brave, what harm can it do?

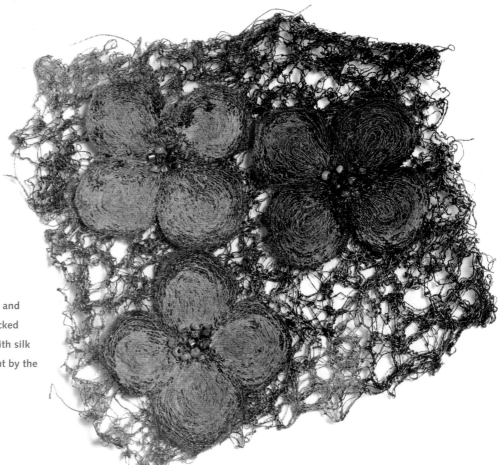

This pretty little piece of water-soluble flowers and lace was stitched in very pale colours which lacked definition. To give it new life, it was dabbed with silk paint and the flowers were given greater weight by the use of acrylic paint.

SECTION 2

This amazing work from Jackie Langfeld is constructed from cardboard, twigs and string. *(Detail below)*

Building up the layers

The previous section should have given some ideas for interesting ground fabric. Now it is time to build on that and add more layers to the work. Mix and match – most background techniques from Section 1 will work with any of the layers in this section. Some of the backgrounds that were featured in the first section need little more in the way of layers to turn them into fully integrated pieces.

Making spines

The pieces on the following pages owe their inspiration to the work of Jackie Langfeld, who produces amazing art using such simple materials as cardboard and string. The formation of 'spines' in her work intrigued me and, with her full permission, I started to explore the formation of spiked ridges in softer surfaces, using fabrics produced in Section 1.

The fabric was pulled up into a pleat to form the spine. Holes were made in the pleat with the point of sharp scissors and, instead of twigs, matchsticks and pipe-cleaners were pushed through the holes.

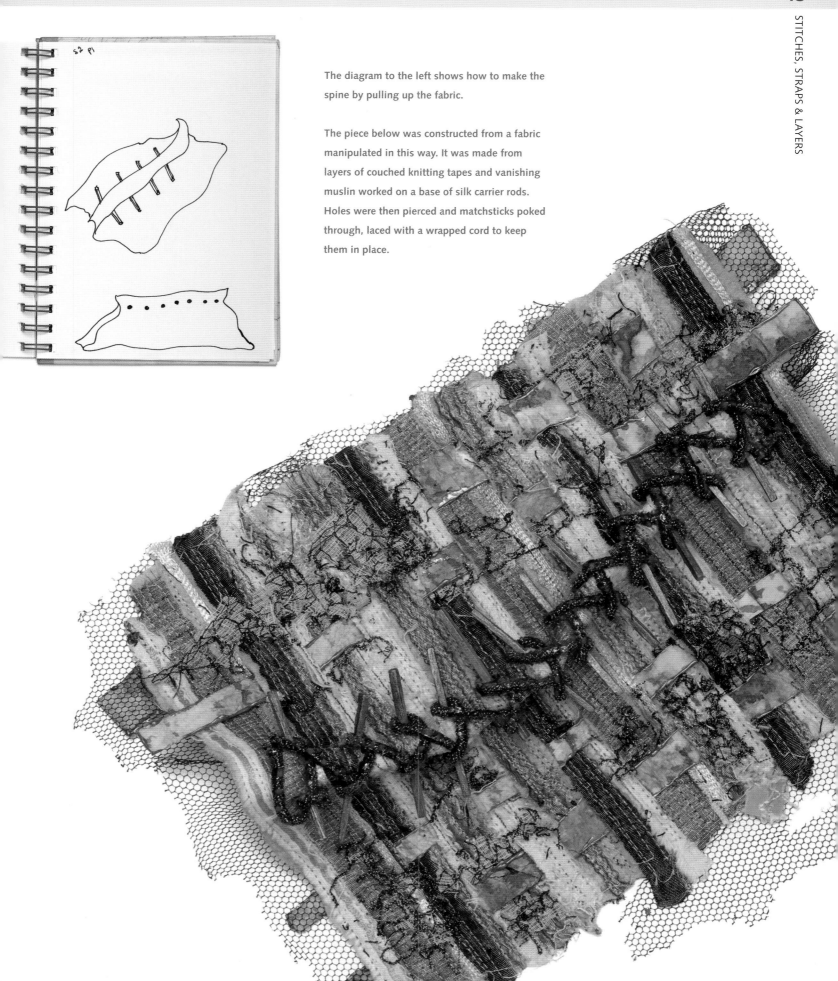

The diagram to the left shows how to make the spine by pulling up the fabric.

The piece below was constructed from a fabric manipulated in this way. It was made from layers of couched knitting tapes and vanishing muslin worked on a base of silk carrier rods. Holes were then pierced and matchsticks poked through, laced with a wrapped cord to keep them in place.

Pipe-cleaners can have beads threaded onto them. Cut the pipe-cleaners into short lengths and wrap them with colourful yarns. Find beads that will fit over the wrapped pipe-cleaners quite firmly and then work as follows:

1 Pull up the fabric to form a spine and make holes through it with a skewer or soldering iron.

2 Push the wrapped pipe-cleaner through the hole in the spine.

3 Thread a bead on each end and push close to the spine to hold the pipe-cleaner in place.

4 Look at the points where the ends of the pipe-cleaners touch – lots of possibilities here for twiddling them together to form new shapes. Have a play.

The background for the pipe-cleaner spine also included a further layer on top of a base of foiled felt and Abaca tissue. It was constructed by making stitched strips – just straight lines of stitch across narrow strips of fabric. Work the technique shown in the sample here like this:

1 Bond a piece of black organza to black muslin (any fine fabrics would work) and draw lines half an inch (about 1 cm) apart.

2 Stitch across the lines – not too heavily – and cut them up.

3 Lay the pieces on the foiled background and place Abaca tissue, chiffon or other fine sheer fabric over the top.

4 Iron, protecting the surface with baking paper. Then pull up into a spine.

TOP: A foiled velvet background which has been overlaid with stitched black organza. This was pinched to form a spine. Beads hold short lengths of pipe-cleaner.

RIGHT: You can see the effect of wrapping the pipe-cleaners.

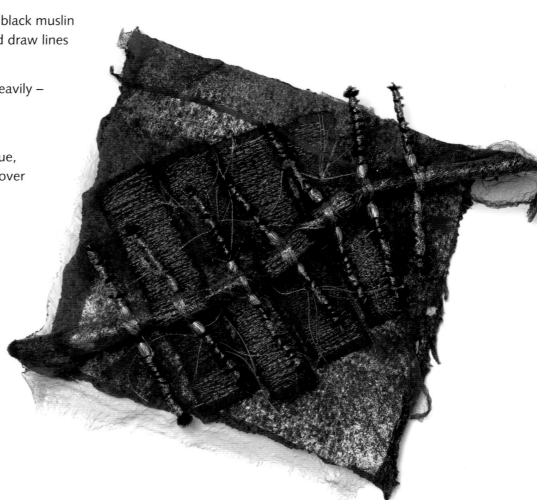

Think of other things that could be pushed through the spine to make it firm and add interest. Lollipop sticks and cocktail sticks are obvious choices but I'm sure you will think of others. All of these are worth considering in their own right too – laid on the fabric and couched down with yarn or wrapped cords.

The spines would be wonderful when used to form the sides of a vessel. Given a firm fabric, they would provide sufficient rigidity to hold it upright. Make three or four rectangles (depending on the shape of the vessel) using one of the background techniques on felt. Add any extra stitching and run a soldering iron along the edges to neaten them. Place the rectangles right sides together, make holes with a soldering iron, then push matchsticks or pipe cleaners through these as before. Wrapped cords hold these together, as you can see in the vessel on the right.

Inside the spine

The spine idea could be reversed – look at the inside of the spine. A deep pleat with coloured bars running across it makes a very interesting dividing device for a panel which would otherwise be static.

A vessel made from machine embroidery on felt. Helmeted warriors are stylized to make a pictorial element. The three stitched panels are then held together by laced matchsticks.

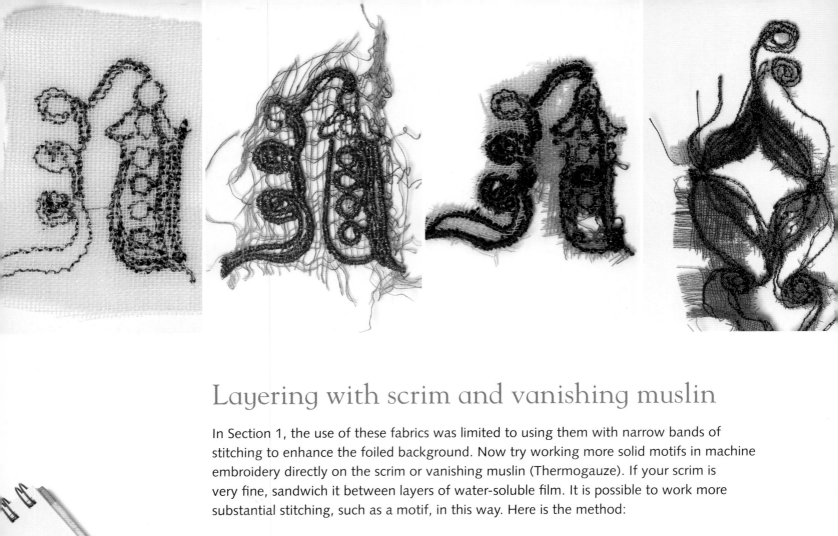

Layering with scrim and vanishing muslin

In Section 1, the use of these fabrics was limited to using them with narrow bands of stitching to enhance the foiled background. Now try working more solid motifs in machine embroidery directly on the scrim or vanishing muslin (Thermogauze). If your scrim is very fine, sandwich it between layers of water-soluble film. It is possible to work more substantial stitching, such as a motif, in this way. Here is the method:

1   Draw the design on a piece of water-soluble film.

2   Make a water-soluble sandwich with the scrim in the middle and the drawing on the top.

3   Stitch, following the design. Bear in mind that the fabric lends itself to outline designs to preserve the fragility of the fabric.

4   Wash away the film.

5   Heat or pull apart to leave the motif with a little of the fabric attached. Stitch this to the background using hand stitches so the fragility is not lost in heavy machining.

The photos on this page show the process of designing and stitching the tiny peapod motif on both scrim and vanishing muslin. An additional motif is also shown. On the opposite page, you can see how these motifs combine to make the bag shown on page 24. This is a detail from the fabric used to make the bag.

Puff paint and embossing powder

For an even more aged effect, try combining either the scrim or the vanishing muslin with puff paint and then heat and paint.

With vanishing muslin, try stamping some motifs (try to get a 'patchy' effect rather than a perfect stamp) on the muslin before heating. Then heat the puff paint and destroy some of the fabric at the same time. Hold the heat tool quite high or use a lower setting if it has one – otherwise you may find that the fabric has disappeared before the paint is puffed. Then proceed as before. You can vary this by sprinkling a little embossing powder onto the wet puff paint. Shake off the excess before heating.

If the scrim is very fine, use two layers and do the stamping and puffing before painting. Then snip some of the fabric close to the motif and pull a few threads away.

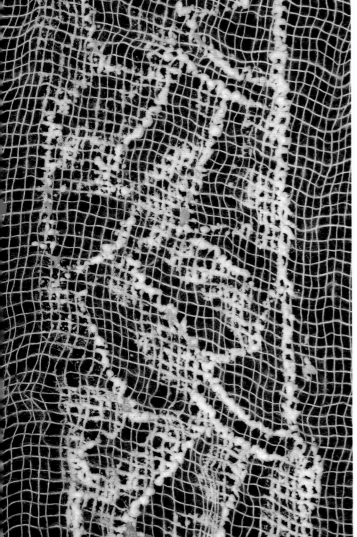

TOP LEFT: Puff paint on vanishing muslin. Some heat has been applied. This makes a very fragile fabric – it could be strengthened by stitching straight lines at half inch intervals before applying paint.

LEFT: Puff paint on scrim.

If the fabric is very crumbly, give it a coating of acrylic wax (matt varnish or Golden Soft Gel, Matte can also be used but acrylic wax is best if you can get it).

Now spray with any paint. You will probably find that the puff paint will be lighter in colour. To avoid this effect, paint with acrylics, being careful with the delicate material. Gild with a dry brush of gold or gold metallic wax when dry.

Bear in mind when attaching the motifs that machining them can flatten and lose the distressed texture. Try hand stitching – just lightly stab stitch to the background. This can look much better.

ABOVE: Vanishing muslin with puff paint was heated, painted and a little wax was applied to the puff paint. It was then hand stitched to foiled velvet.

LEFT: The back of a book-cover showing puff painted vanishing muslin over foiled velvet. This was machine stitched to apply it to the velvet. The motif was outlined felt using the techniques described on the next page.

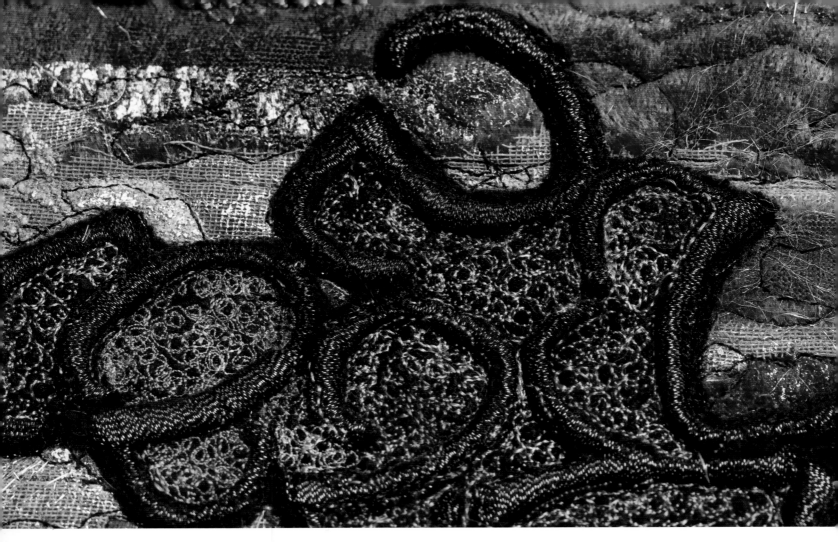

Felt motifs

This technique involves a lot of stitching, cutting and applying but the final result is well worth it. It gives a really raised outline that can be filled in a wide variety of ways.

The idea is that you select an outline design, like the one shown here, stitch it on felt using your widest satin stitch and then cut it out. It is then applied to another piece of felt and the centres are stitched. Cut out again and apply to the chosen background.

TOP: Detail of the book cover shown on the previous page. Shapes were stitched on black felt, cut out and then placed on another piece of felt where centres were machine embroidered. Finally the whole thing was cut out and stitched to the background. This gives a solid raised motif.

RIGHT: A photograph of clematis had its colours changed using a paint program. The shapes of the petals were isolated and sample sketches made to isolate outlines for the felt technique.

Here is the method in more detail:

1 Either work motifs on felt freehand, choosing simple shapes (leaves or geometric shapes) or trace the design on tissue and stitch onto felt using free running stitch. Tear away the tissue when the design is transferred.

To form motifs:

2 Stitch a linear outline pattern on felt, using a zigzag satin stitch set at a width of around 6 (or your widest setting). Close up the stitch length for a solid satin stitch. These outlines are best stitched with metallic thread. See the note on page 52 for hints on stitching.

3 Cut out the outline, leaving a narrow border of felt around the stitching. If acrylic felt has been used a soldering iron could be a fast method of isolating the motifs. Work in a well-ventilated area and take great care not to burn yourself – remember that the felt will be very hot.

4 Lay the outlines on another piece of felt and stitch the inner area of the cut-out to the base, using an embroidery thread that matches the felt. Change to a colourful thread, perhaps a variegated shade. Fill the inner space with stitch, working small circles or solid ones (granite stitch).

5 When finished, cut out the new motifs and place them on a suitable background. Stitch into place around the outside of the motif.

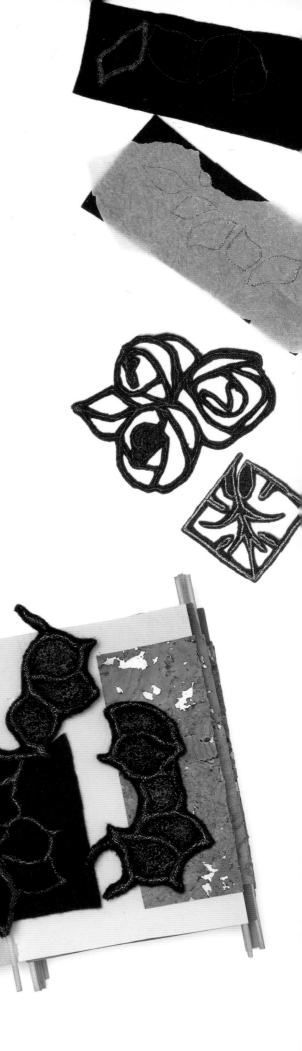

ABOVE RIGHT: Here you can see the process of drawing the design on tissue and stitching it.

RIGHT: A book of samples showing how the outline is placed on more felt and stitched, resulting in the cut-out motif. On the right of the book page, the centres were filled with stitch on water-soluble film.

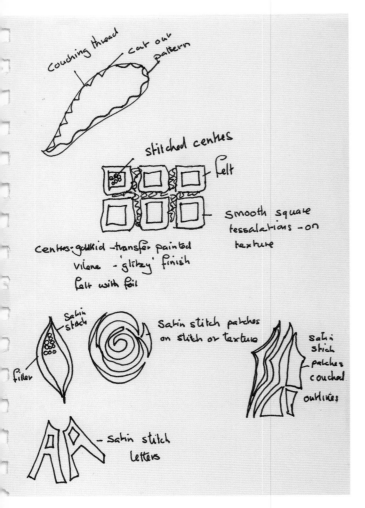

Couching thread — Cut out pattern

stitched centres — felt

Centres: goldkid—transfer painted Vilene – 'glitzy' finish felt with foil

Smooth square tessalations – on texture

Satin stitch — Filler

Satin stitch patches on stitch or texture

Satin stitch patches couched outlines

Satin stitch Letters

ABOVE: Sketch book page showing doodles of shapes that might be suitable for felt cut-outs.

RIGHT: These cut-outs, on walnut inked felt, show the beginning of cable stitch fillings. Both straight lines and circles are shown. They would need lots more stitching to fill the shapes. This gives excellent texture.

NOTE ON STITCHING THE OUTLINES

Consider a shape such as a leaf. When stitching the outline of the leaf using satin stitch, you could move the fabric around to follow the stitching. This gives an even result but needs care in the stitching. Alternatively, try using 'cheat's' satin stitch where the fabric is not turned as the stitch is formed. This gives a calligraphic effect with some lines thinner at the turns. Practise both effects – they're very good for improving control when stitching.

ALTERNATIVE FILLINGS

Other fillings could be considered for the centre of the shapes. Try:

- whip stitch – tighten the top thread

- cable stitch – turn the work upside down and use a heavy thread on the bobbin (use the stitched outlines as a guide for stitching)

- lay the cut-out felt (stage 3) onto water-soluble fabric or film placed in a hoop. Stitch around the edge to secure it to the film and then work free running stitch for a lacy effect in the centre. Do make sure that the stitches overlap so that they don't unravel when the film is dissolved. Dissolve as usual, pull into shape and leave to dry on a flat surface. Place on a background or join motifs together for a lacy piece of work.

It is also possible to couch the stitched outline over solid machine embroidery – perhaps a shapeless sample from the failed embroidery box.

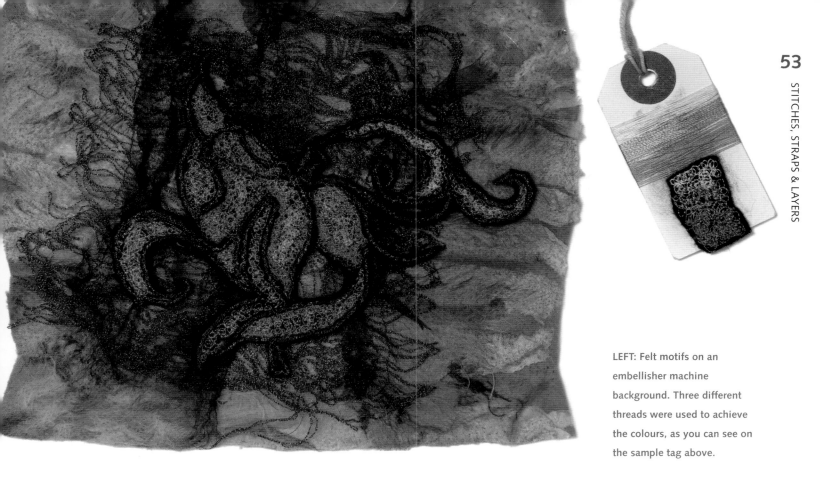

LEFT: Felt motifs on an embellisher machine background. Three different threads were used to achieve the colours, as you can see on the sample tag above.

RIGHT: A book made using this technique. The cut-outs were placed on a paper background.

OUTLINES WITH METAL CENTRES

REUSE & SAVE

The cut-out felt can be stitched to metal foil or shim, or perhaps try the inside of tomato purée tubes for this rich metallic effect. It is best used on a sumptuous background – something like richly foiled velvet. If you are using shim, it can be coloured first by holding it in a flame.

Work like this:

1   Choose a suitable design. Work satin stitch and cut out the felt as before (stage 3, page 51). Or use the 'quick-strip' (page 57) method and just produce a long satin stitch strip.

2   Place a piece of fine metal shim or recycled tube on a firm base such as pelmet Vilene.

3   Lay the cut-out felt on top and stitch around all the edges of the felt, inside and out, using a thread that matches the colour of the felt.

4   Cut out the motif carefully – the metal can be sharp. When cut out, go around the outer edges again snipping the metal right back to the stitching.

5   Draw into the metal centres using an embossing tool or an old ballpoint pen. The usual way to emboss metal means working from the back but this technique is easier from the right side.

6   Paint over the metal with dark acrylic paint and wipe off immediately, allowing some of the paint to remain in the dips. This ages the metal and takes some of the overpowering brightness away.

The piece can then be applied to a background or used alone as a 'corsage'. A vase full of metal flowers made using this technique would be fun.

A figured velvet was foiled and stitched for this background. Felt cut-outs were stitched to metal for the side panels and stitched directly to the velvet. A metal 'corsage' of leaves forms the centre piece. The whole piece was stitched to Wireform and then backed with felt. This enables it to be given a moulded shape.

Solid motifs – couched edges

The previous techniques work well because the cut-out felt outline defines a shape and the interior stitching provides a contrast. It is, however, possible to enhance solidly stitched shapes by couching heavy threads or wrapped cords around them. This could be done with a solid motif as the central theme. Free machine on the felt and cut out, leaving a small area of felt around the shape. Couch a thread such as a weighty gimp or a metal thread around the edge and then trim back. Apply to the background.

LEFT: A variety of motifs, some with couched edges.

OPPOSITE: Lutradur on felt with some straight line stitching and zapping. White silk forms a centrepiece for stitched net. Applied to this base are water-soluble squares (see page 63) and domes made from moulded metal shim. The finishing touch is a motif made from manipulated satin stitch strips.

REALLY EASY OUTLINES

OK, so that's one way to do it but here's an idea for a really quick and simple outlining method. Working on felt, as before:

1 Stitch a long strip of satin stitch – set the width to about 5 for the first experiment. Close it up to get a really even stitch and just keep going.

2 Fasten off at the end of the strip and then cut out – quite close to the stitching but not so close that you'll clip the thread.

3 Hand-stitch the strip to a background fabric, working it in close circles and stab stitching to hold the strip to the ground fabric.

4 Work spirals, squares, Art Nouveau roses – get adventurous. This is fantastic for cushions or book-covers.

ABOVE: On the left of the pic, you can see the straight line of satin stitch and, on the right, motifs made by manipulating them.

Paper-based motifs

   I vowed that there would be no reference to water-soluble paper in this book but I have found such a good money-saving tip that I have been forced to include it. There is also the fact that cast paper motifs are great for building up backgrounds or, indeed, for providing focal points for wall-hung work.

Here is my money-saving tip, discovered by students working from the last book: use toilet paper instead of expensive dissolvable paper. However, I was disappointed in the result as it seemed to me that the definition was not good. The whole delight of water-soluble paper is the very sharp detail that can be achieved. The answer, of course, is obvious: use a little water-soluble paper next to the mould and then fill with toilet paper. It works. I'll describe it step by step, including the method for making the mould from Softsculpt – this is Jane Wild's invention from our *Paper, Metal and Stitch* book.

Choose a suitable object to use as a mould. We want something with a bit of depth and lots of detail. Start with something simple, and practise.

1   Lay the object down close to the oven and then heat the Softsculpt, paying particular attention to the temperature instructions on the pack. It goes floppy when warm but should not be too hot to handle.

2   Whip it out of the oven and, very quickly, press it hard onto your object. If it doesn't work, warm it up and try again.

3   Work on the inside of the mould where the detail is to be found. Lay some scraps of dissolvable paper in the mould and wet them with a paintbrush until mushy. Spread a thin layer of wet pulp over the base of the mould and allow to dry for a few hours – don't put it anywhere warm to dry.

4   Then wet the toilet paper in a bowl to reduce it to something close to pulp. Squeeze the water out and press the pulpy remains on top of the partly dried dissolvable paper.

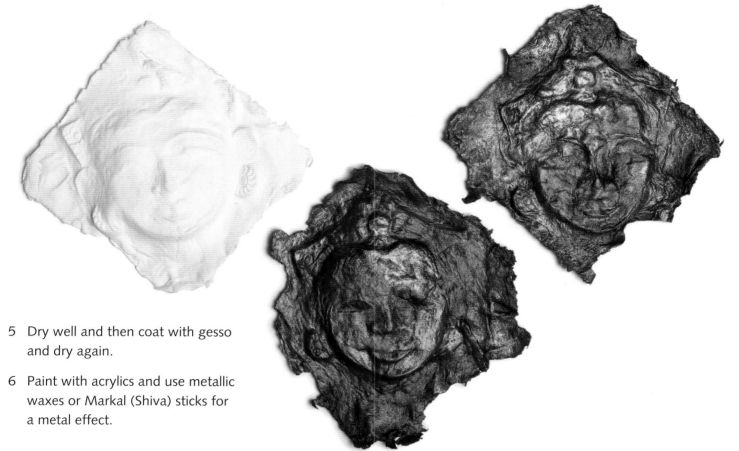

5 Dry well and then coat with gesso and dry again.

6 Paint with acrylics and use metallic waxes or Markal (Shiva) sticks for a metal effect.

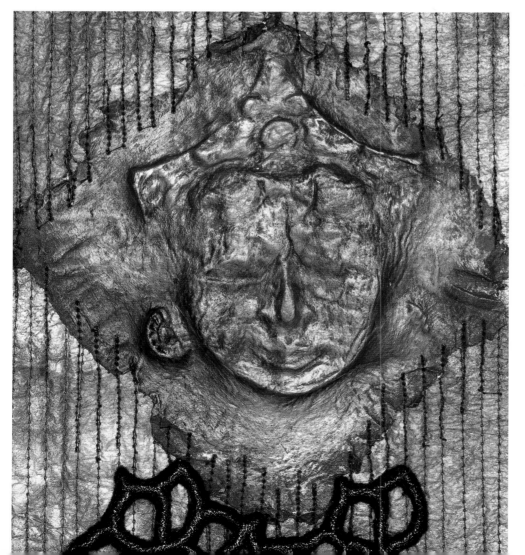

ABOVE: At the top are cast paper shapes from another Buddha mould. These were painted with burnt umber and then, when that was dry, waxed to give a metallic gleam and left for a few days. Finally, they were painted with Golden Quinacridone fluid paints.

LEFT: Here you can see the finished face stitched to a background of bonded tissue paper.

OPPOSITE: (TOP) This Buddha was used to mould Softsculpt into a face shape. (BOTTOM) The resulting cast paper shape was made from a little water-soluble paper and a lot of soft toilet paper.

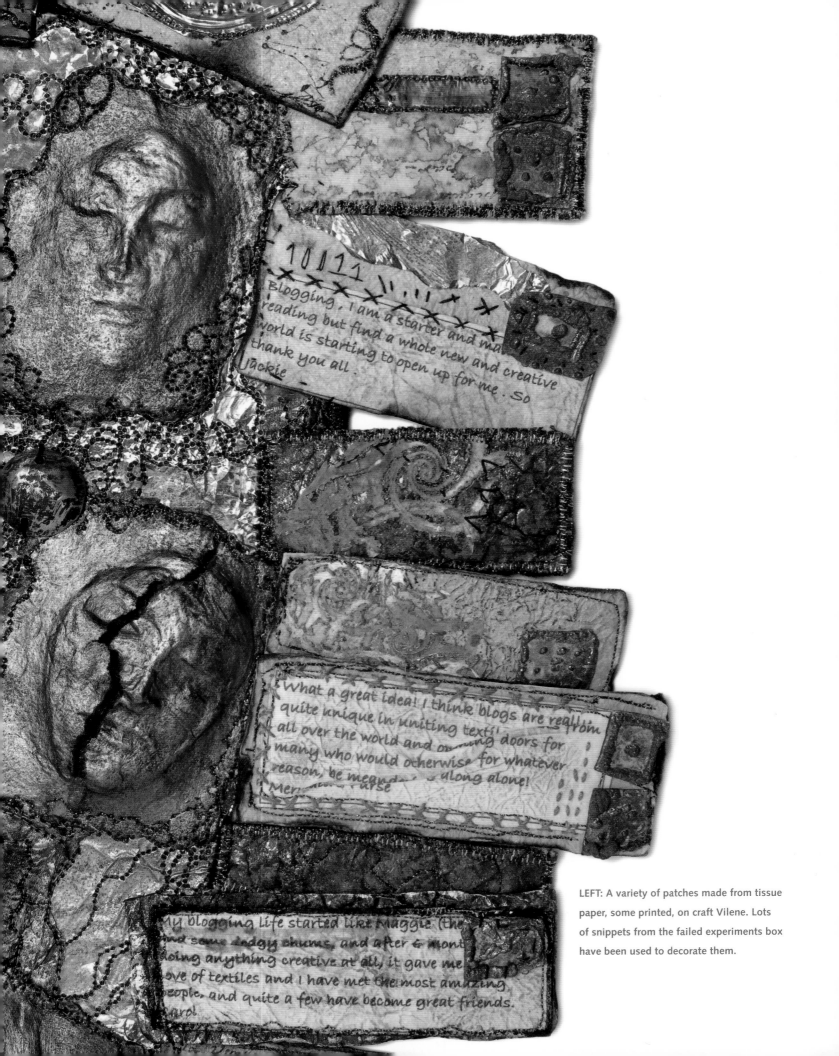

10011

Blogging, I am a starter and ma... reading but find a whole new and creative world is starting to open up for me. So thank you all.
Jackie

What a great idea! I think blogs are really quite unique in uniting texti... ...from all over the world and o...ing doors for many who would otherwise for whatever reason, be mean... ...along alone!
Mer... ...urse

My blogging life started like Maggie (the... ...nd some odd[g]y chums, and after 6 mont... ...doing anything creative at all, it gave me... ...ove of textiles and I have met the most amazing ...cople, and quite a few have become great friends. ...aro[l.]

LEFT: A variety of patches made from tissue paper, some printed, on craft Vilene. Lots of snippets from the failed experiments box have been used to decorate them.

Patches

Patches are a general term for small, usually geometric, pieces made separately and applied to a piece of work. I often use this technique around the perimeter of a piece, as it deals with the tricky subject of edges and borders on paper-based work which is sometimes unsuitable for other approaches.

Here is the basic method:

1   Bond crumpled tissue to craft Vilene. Recycled tissue from shoeboxes is great.

2   Paint with tea, coffee or walnut ink.

3   Cut some strips from this. They will form borders for the patches.

4   Cut the rest of the piece into random shapes, roughly rectangular.

5   Decorate in any way you like. Ideas are given on page 62.

6   To finish you can stitch around the edges of the patch with a line or two of straight stitch and then burn the edges. Or edge with satin stitch, form borders from narrow strips of tissue and Vilene or use dimension paint or embossing powder.

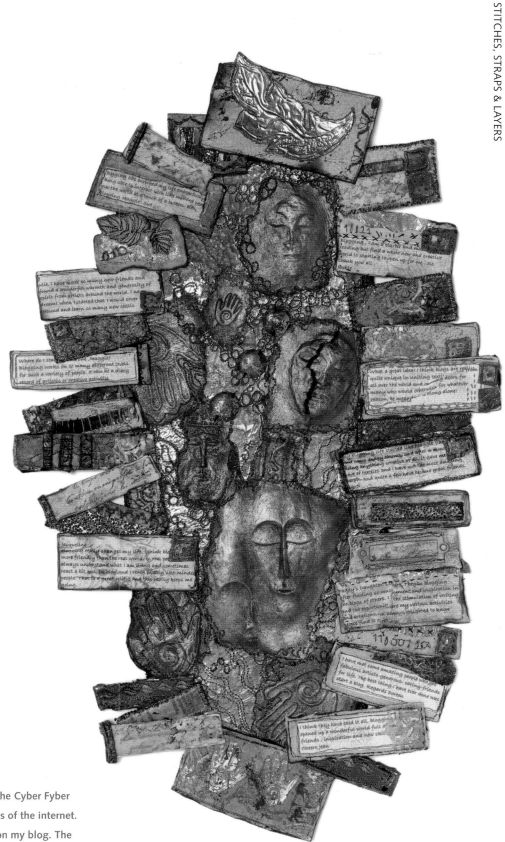

RIGHT: 'Binary Humanity'. This textile was made for the Cyber Fyber exhibition in the USA which celebrated the advantages of the internet. The patches around the edges contain messages left on my blog. The centre is formed from cast paper, metal shim and stitch. Some papers by Jane Wild.

Decorating the patch

Now it's up to you – use lettering, stamping, pieces of metal shim, snippets from the failed experiments box, charms, beads – endless possibilities.

Consider using some bright colours that tone or contrast with the background. You may have a theme or a message in the main textile that can be explained or expanded using the patches.

ABOVE: A patch decorated with a metal shim leaf.

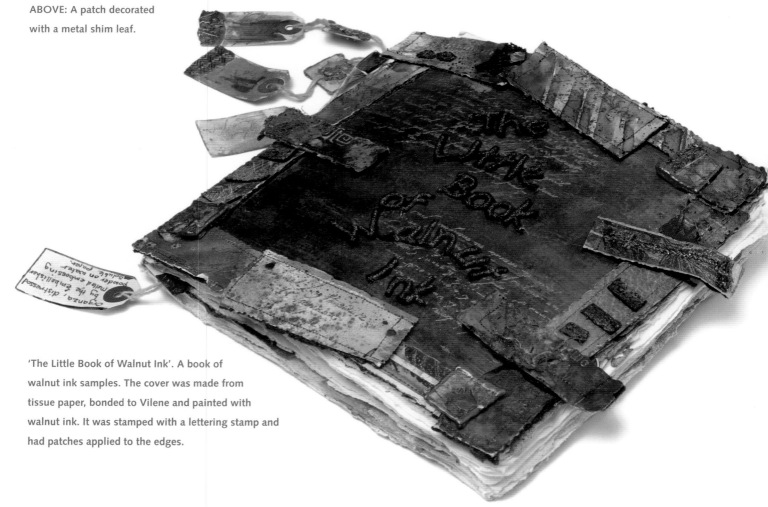

'The Little Book of Walnut Ink'. A book of walnut ink samples. The cover was made from tissue paper, bonded to Vilene and painted with walnut ink. It was stamped with a lettering stamp and had patches applied to the edges.

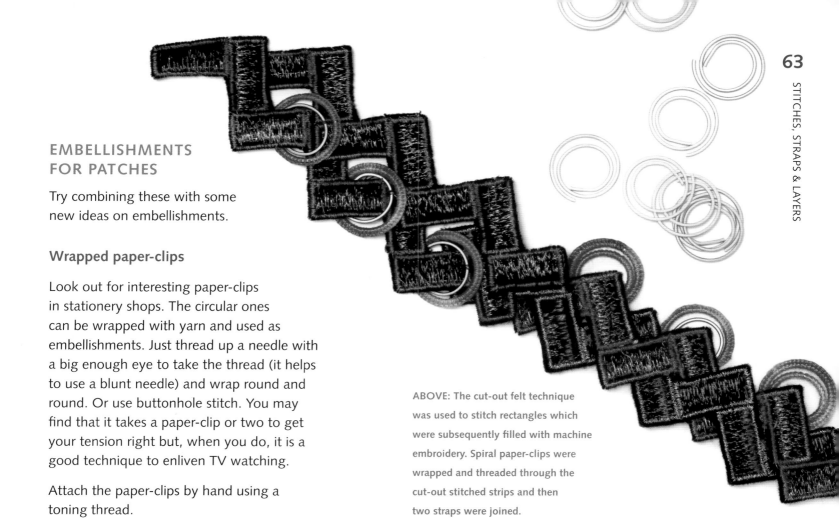

EMBELLISHMENTS FOR PATCHES

Try combining these with some new ideas on embellishments.

Wrapped paper-clips

Look out for interesting paper-clips in stationery shops. The circular ones can be wrapped with yarn and used as embellishments. Just thread up a needle with a big enough eye to take the thread (it helps to use a blunt needle) and wrap round and round. Or use buttonhole stitch. You may find that it takes a paper-clip or two to get your tension right but, when you do, it is a good technique to enliven TV watching.

Attach the paper-clips by hand using a toning thread.

ABOVE: The cut-out felt technique was used to stitch rectangles which were subsequently filled with machine embroidery. Spiral paper-clips were wrapped and threaded through the cut-out stitched strips and then two straps were joined.

ABOVE: Water-soluble film was heavily machined with little squares. It was stitched again, across the initial stitching, to prevent unravelling. When the film was dissolved (pin down each square or it will float away), they curled and made fat little cushions.

Raised squares

1 Draw a series of squares on water-soluble film. The heavier film works best here as a little film should remain in the square to shape it.
2 Fill the squares with free machine straight stitching until the shape is filled. The stitching should be quite heavy. Stitch a final row diagonally, in the other direction, to lock the stitching.
3 Cut out the squares and dissolve. Leave enough film in so that the shape is not floppy – but not enough to show 'snail's trails'.
4 Stitch several together on a patch to add impact.

Puff paint embellishments

Try these tiny patches of puff paint – they're quick to make and look great. Here's how:

1   Place puff paint in a squeezy bottle and pipe onto a scrap of Vilene, as shown below.

2   Sprinkle some embossing powder on top and puff with a heat tool.

3   Paint inside with metallic paints or spray with Adirondack washes.

4   Add a little metallic wax, if needed.

5   Cut from the Vilene and apply by hand or machine.

All of these ideas can, of course, be used in many other ways and the water-soluble shapes can be rectangles or triangles, too.

Metal patches

Patches, used where the edges form an important part of the work, have served me well and this technique can be extended by making motifs from metal shim or tomato purée tubes. You can see how effective this is in the piece on the right.

In this alms bag made by Hazel Credland, metal has been sensitively used throughout. Particular attention has been given to the edges, where the metal patch holds a tassel. Hazel's design book is shown below – here inkjet transparencies aid design by overlapping to help decide the placement of the pieces.

There are lots of ideas in this section for building up textiles. Many can be used just as they are but the next section contains even more ideas for using the layering process to great effect.

I could decide which shapes held the most importance

Strips and straps

Strips of material can also be used to build up layers and, when applied to a background, give either a pleasing continuity of pattern or a wild, riotous – apparently random – effect. Strips turn into straps that can be applied to fabric, built into vessels or used as belts, bag handles or facings for wearable art.

In this section you'll find exciting ideas for a variety of bands – some paper, some embellished and some stitched. These can stand alone as edging devices or can be couched all over a background for a bag or book-cover. They are great when woven on small looms, especially when these have warps made from wrapped pipe-cleaners.

Materials

REUSE & SAVE

A general point about making straps is that the process is much quicker when using ready-made strips – sari strips, ribbons, silk pods and so on. Of course, it's quite simple to cut and tear your own fabric (and would use up the stash very effectively) but do the cutting or tearing first as there is something immensely satisfying in just grabbing a handful of colourful lengths and getting straight into the making process.

Making the straps

Here are some ideas we shall be exploring for the bands:

- strips of sari silk applied to felt with the embellisher and then cut up

- embellished surfaces – silk or wool fibres with chiffon, perhaps on scrim

- paper, stamped, stencilled and painted – this can be stitched to felt to make it stronger

- carrier rods, split and applied to felt, combined with couched thread

- flower-stitched circles or cut-out patterns with wrapped cords running through them

- pieces of embellished fabric and cut-out pieces of embroidery stitched onto water-soluble fabric or net

- wrapped rings or paper-clips enhancing a stitched strap

- stitched border patterns cut from felt and enhanced by further stitching on water-soluble fabric

- flat knitting tapes embellished or stitched make a great base.

Some of these ideas can be seen here.

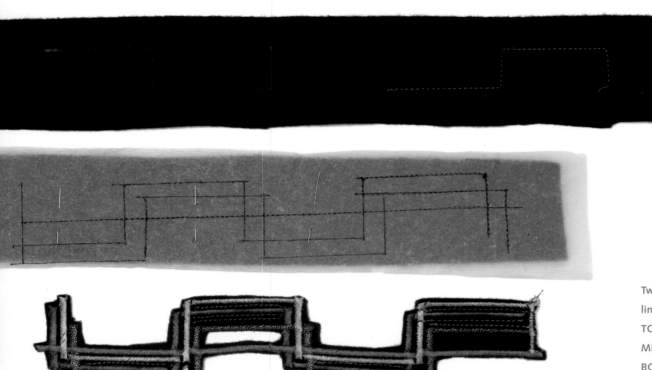

Two methods of transferring the linear design.
TOP: Lines drawn with chalk.
MIDDLE: Lines drawn on tissue.
BOTTOM: Stitched lines on felt, partially cut out.

Basic straps

Straps are good to make, relatively fast to produce and strangely satisfying to handle. This section of the book is divided into parts that cover:

- making a series of basic straps using a variety of materials and methods

- couching techniques to enhance these straps – what to use and how to use (and abuse) it

- edgings – the finishing touch.

Stitched straps

1 Draw a geometric pattern on tissue. Place the tissue on felt and straight stitch with the foot on and the feed dogs up. Tear tissue away.

2 Stitch on the other side of the felt, using a fairly substantial satin stitch. Try different widths or vary the width in the same strap. Cut out.

3 Apply to a background.

BELOW: The stitched strap shown on page 69 is laid over a stencilled paper strap.

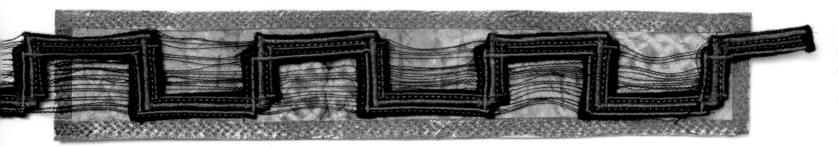

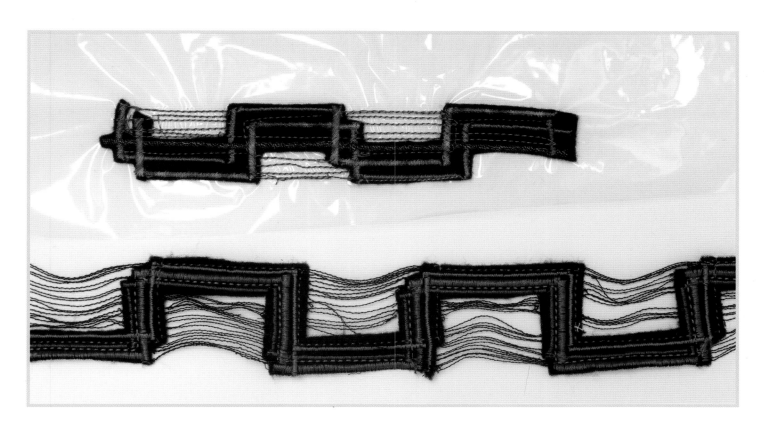

Although the method described here uses an initial design, this technique can also be worked 'freehand' by marking areas along the strap.

1   Cut a strip of felt and, using tailor's chalk, draw lines across and down at regular intervals – say 1¹/₂ in. (4 cm).

2   Straight stitch down the line first and then satin stitch, as shown.

3   Work additional lines on this base. Vary the satin stitch by using a thicker thread with straight stitch.

This strap can be placed over a background, wrapped around a book as a closing device or used as an edging for clothing. It can also be enhanced by adding elements of water-soluble stitching.

ABOVE and RIGHT: The stitched and cut strap is placed on water-soluble film and straight lines are stitched in the spaces.

Water-soluble straps

Water-soluble film or fabric is a useful material, both for adding to straps and for building up new ones. The technique above for the stitched straps can be extended with the use of this material. Just lay the strap on water-soluble fabric and stitch some lacy bits or extra lines. Dissolve.

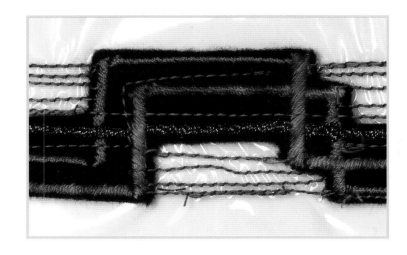

The water-soluble trick can also be used to join more solid areas, such as the small square 'patches' shown below. The patches are simply squares made from foiled felt with flat knitting tape stitched to them. They could be off-cuts from a larger piece and would work well as other shapes, too. Pinned to the water-soluble fabrics, they are joined using further knitting tape, overstitched with zigzag. Then straight stitch can be worked to join all the elements together.

Small squares of stitched fabric were placed on water-soluble film. These were stitched to attach them to the couched yarns. The result is shown below.

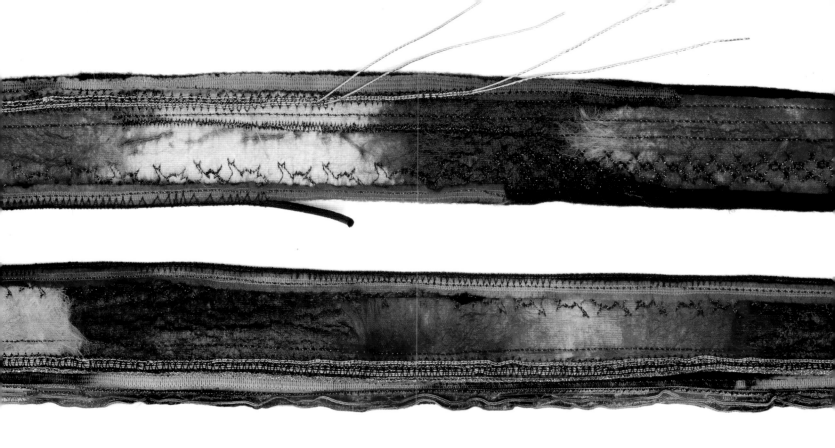

The stages of stitching are shown at the top, where the carrier rods have been stitched to the background and the couched yarns are being applied. The finished strap is shown in the middle pic. The bottom pic shows how motifs stitched on felt can add the final touch.

Carrier rod straps

We've used these rods to make backgrounds but they are also great for straps.

1   Cut the felt, as before, into strips, slightly wider than required.

2   Split the pods into layers. If you are planning to use the resulting straps for a vessel, do not split into more than two layers or it will be too floppy.

3   Stitch the pods to the felt using the normal presser foot and straight stitch. Use a stitch guide or the edge of the felt to keep you straight. If the strap is buckled, press under baking paper to flatten.

4   Couch lengths of colourful yarn or knitting tapes along the sides of the carrier rods – see notes on couching, page 84.

5   Add couched metal threads. Really cheap ones such as the slightly stretchy Christmas wrappings can be used. However, for a really glitzy effect, you can't beat jap gold which gives a real zing.

Detail of 'Celtic Pod' from page 5, showing how the
carrier rod straps have been manipulated to form a vessel.

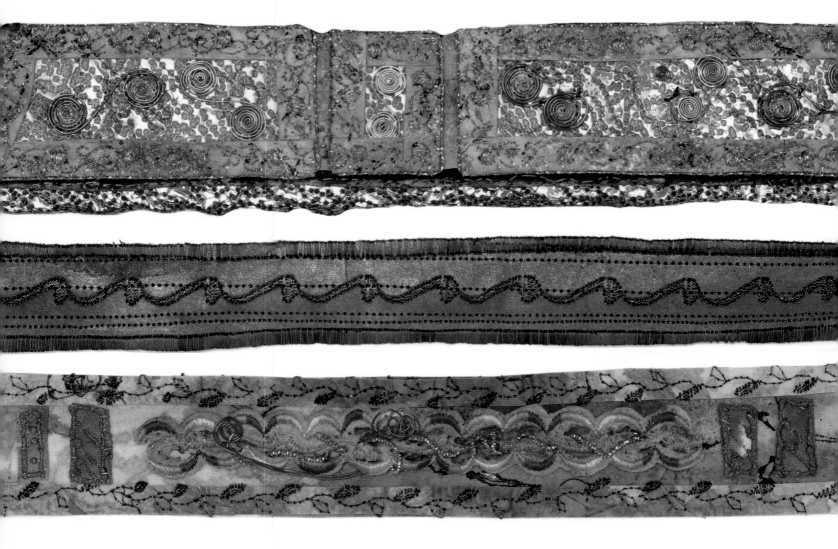

Paper straps

As discussed in Section 2, paper textiles offer the chance to use all the wonderful paint products which never work so well on fabric. This also applies to straps. Try:

- bonding Abaca tissue to strips of felt or craft Vilene and painting with Adirondack sprays, walnut ink, Moon Shadow Mists etc.

- stitching heavyweight watercolour paper to strips of felt – great for vessels

- dabbing black puff paint onto one of these surfaces then sprinkling with embossing powder and puffing with a heat tool

- adding printed elements – these could be as simple as a piece of Abaca tissue with a hand-written note, or could be designs prepared on the computer.

Three paper straps.

TOP: Stitched metal purée tube is edged with thin borders of painted craft Vilene. Curled wires were added.

MIDDLE: Straight lines of stitching are covered with a single line of pattern stitch.

BOTTOM: A paper strap, coloured with walnut ink. Cut out pattern stitches were applied to the strap.

Printed designs

A strap could form the central area of a narrow piece of work, giving it a prominence and turning it into a focal point. Computer-printed tissue paper could be used, like this:

1   Cut Abaca tissue slightly larger than a piece of printer paper.

2   Use a glue stick around the edge of the printer paper and then press the tissue onto the glue. It should be firmly attached all around.

3   Print as a single sheet, watching it carefully as it goes through.

I've never had any trouble using this method but don't use it with a laser printer.

The background of this piece uses four paper straps stitched to a gold painted fabric. The focal point is made from computer printed tissue bonded to Vilene. Scraps of cast paper were used to integrate the fish into the background.

The straps shown above cover a variety of techniques from stencilling to the use of stamps and embossing powder. They are described below from left to right:

- Paper beads were formed by wrapping jap gold around a matchstick. Triangles of painted paper were glued to the matchstick and rolled up to form the bead.

- Painted watercolour paper was stamped with gold ink and enhanced with embossing powder. The edges were decorated with a previously stitched ribbon and couched metallic thread. Finally paper beads were added.

- Stamped puff paint was sprinkled with embossing powder before expanding it with a heat tool. The borders were made from craft Vilene and stitched to the base using a pattern stitch.

- Stencilled tissue paper was bonded to Vilene and torn scraps of tissue stamped with text were glued over the stencils.

- Mono-printed watercolour paper was stitched with an appliqué stitch. This is shown part-stitched.

- Thin slivers of carrier rod were applied to painted watercolour paper with a temporary adhesive. This was then stitched using straight lines.

This icon used an image of a saint, printed on tissue
paper. Paper straps formed a frame for the central motif
and were enhanced by machine and hand stitching.
Painted Japanese paper was applied to add colour.

Fabric straps

The stamping technique discussed earlier is very suitable for fabric straps. Work in the same way as the paper but with painted or dyed fabric as a base, altering the size of the strip of fabric and, perhaps, using two stamps. Join the strips together to make cushions, book covers or wearable art.

This jacket by Elli Woodsford was constructed entirely of joined straps. These started life as dyed fabric which was printed with gold acrylic paint, using a wooden block. The printed fabric was torn into a variety of widths which altered the scale of the motif and made it appear much more interesting. The jacket is quite a structured garment and the fact that acrylic paint was used does not affect the handle of the fabric. The strips were joined together into layered straps and stitched together before the pattern pieces were pinned on. At this point the pattern was adjusted to allow for the staggered edges around the bottom.

Embellisher machine straps

The embellisher machine is great for straps. Try working small pieces of stitching onto an already embellished ground, or applying motifs made by one of the methods in Section 2 to an embellished strip. Even better, use any off-cuts from the carrier rod straps.

EMBELLISHED STITCHING

The embellisher machine can be used in many ways, perhaps to apply the stitched straps from page 68 to a background. Working over the stitching with the machine can soften and blend it for interesting results. The water-soluble stitching will probably not embellish but will lie on the surface, held securely by the embellished felt.

Fibres embellished over felt also make good strips, especially when enhanced with further decorations.

A variety of straps made using the embellisher machine.

SARI STRIPS

These are ready-torn strips made from sari fabrics. They are different from the sari ribbons, which have finished edges – these are satisfyingly ragged. They work really well when embellished onto felt, especially when couched yarns and metal threads are stitched as edgings.

It's best to cut the felt strips a little wider than required as it's easier to embellish and then stitch. If you need a lot of strips they can be worked side by side and cut out afterwards.

Just embellish them to felt (if you are lucky, some of the silks will have little patterns which add interest). Then couch yarns alongside them – see note below.

If you don't have an embellisher machine, these can be stitched down with straight lines.

VELVET RIBBON STRAPS

Use these in exactly the same way as the sari strips – just embellish and then add couched threads, particularly the flat knitting tapes. Consider cutting the ribbons into squares or rectangles and working on foiled felt. Couch around the squares.

A foiled background is used with these sari strips and applied using the embellisher machine.

Couching

Whichever method you use to make the basic straps they will be enhanced by couched thread. I have two particular favourites: metallic threads and flat knitting tapes.

The knitting tapes are such good value and will last forever – they come in fantastic colours, too. For all the work in this book, I've just used two hanks – one with blues (turquoise to navy) and one pink (corals through to reds). There always seemed to be just the right colour somewhere in the hank.

The metal threads used here range from jap gold to Christmas tape. Mixing a shiny gold with a matt one gives a good contrast. Other yarns and threads to look out for range from dyed gimp – which comes in a variety of weights – to ribbons or knitting yarns. Don't overlook the thinner yarns which can be plaited or stitched together before couching to a background.

FEET

It is very likely that your machine will have a special foot for couching. Some have a special facility for feeding the thread through evenly. Look out for a braiding foot but don't despair if you haven't got one – a wide-toed foot or a standard foot can be used. In some cases using the wrong foot gives quite interesting results.

A variety of yarns applied to a foiled background are shown opposite. On this page you can see how using the correct foot on the sewing machine makes the couching process much easier.

STITCHING

Here are some things to consider:

- Does the fabric you're working on need a stabiliser? Felt will give no problems but lighter fabrics will buckle.

- Which colour will you use for the top thread? Perhaps a variegated would look good – or should you try a contrast or one that tones with the yarn to be couched?

- Will you work straight lines with the feed dogs raised or use free machine techniques?

Some sampling may be required to help you decide. Keep all these samples in a book with notes. It's so useful to be able to look back and we all tend to forget unless notes are made.

Having made these decisions, the basic stitching is simple. Select satin stitch with a width that just covers the thread you are couching without catching it. The amount of coverage – how close the stitches are – is really up to you. With something like jap gold, it can be quite closed up and still show a lovely golden gleam. Or maybe you want more of the yarn showing, in which case keep it wide.

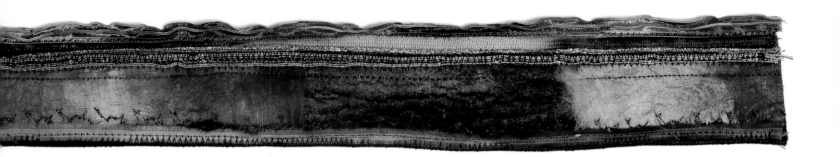

Edging and finishing

Different edgings can affect the look of a strap. For example, a crisp sharp effect can be obtained by simply over-sewing with satin stitch along the edges of the strip. Or for a soft frilly result use one of the loose-edged knitting yarns, stitched along the edge with a straight stitch.

For a really sharp, well-defined edge, use the black rat's tail braid, often sold as jewellery thongs. It is possible to buy these in a variety of colours as leather thongs and, for a special piece, this would look good.

Rat's tail braid edges the strap on the left. It continues over the edge to form ties with carrier rod tassels. The strap above uses a buckled yarn to give a 'frilly' edge.

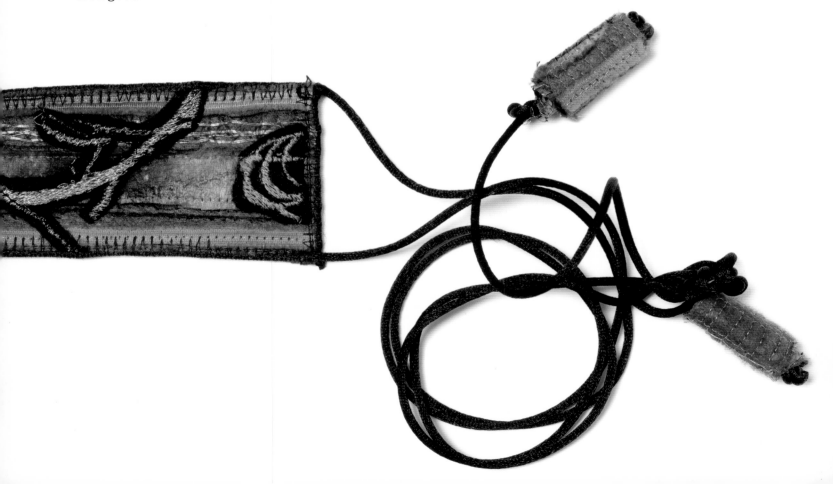

For a more abstract effect, use one of the beaded sticky ribbons available for card-makers and scrap-bookers. Try painting with acrylics and then wiping off some of the paint – this will antique the over-bright gold. Another fun option is to squash down a little water-soluble paper (toilet paper is a bit too thick for this technique) over the top of the beads. Keep it a very fine layer and paint when dry.

The horrid sticky ribbon below is stitched to the strap. It is then covered with water-soluble paper and painted with a dilute walnut ink wash to tone with the Lutradur background of the strap. Stamped polymer clay provided the motif. *(Samantha Packer)*

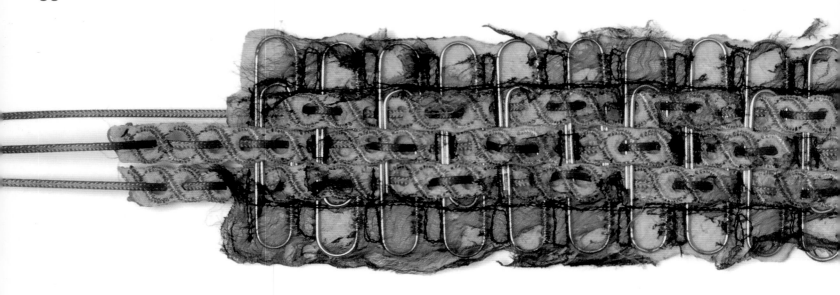

The final touch

Beads, applied motifs, even paper-clips – all kinds of bits and pieces will add embellishment to the basic straps. Also consider the water-soluble squares shown in Section 2 (page 63).

Consider stitched motifs that could go on top. You may decide that you like your strap exactly as it is but, if it needs a little extra 'oomph', look back at some of the motifs that were created to build up the layers. Free-machined motifs on net or felt can be stitched onto the strap to add interest. Best of all, you can make them and try them in various places to see where they look best.

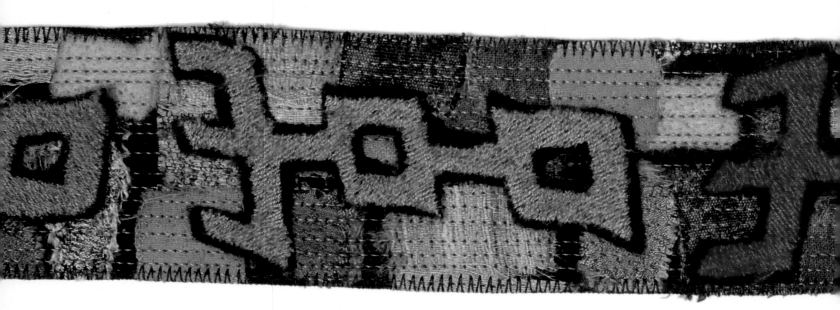

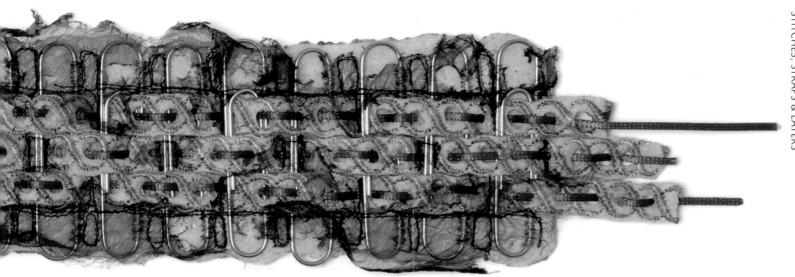

ABOVE: Ordinary paper-clips with braid
threaded through them make a fun strap.

BELOW: Carrier rods, pulled into small pieces,
make a backdrop to the cut-out motifs on this
strap. *(Valerie Campbell-Harding)*

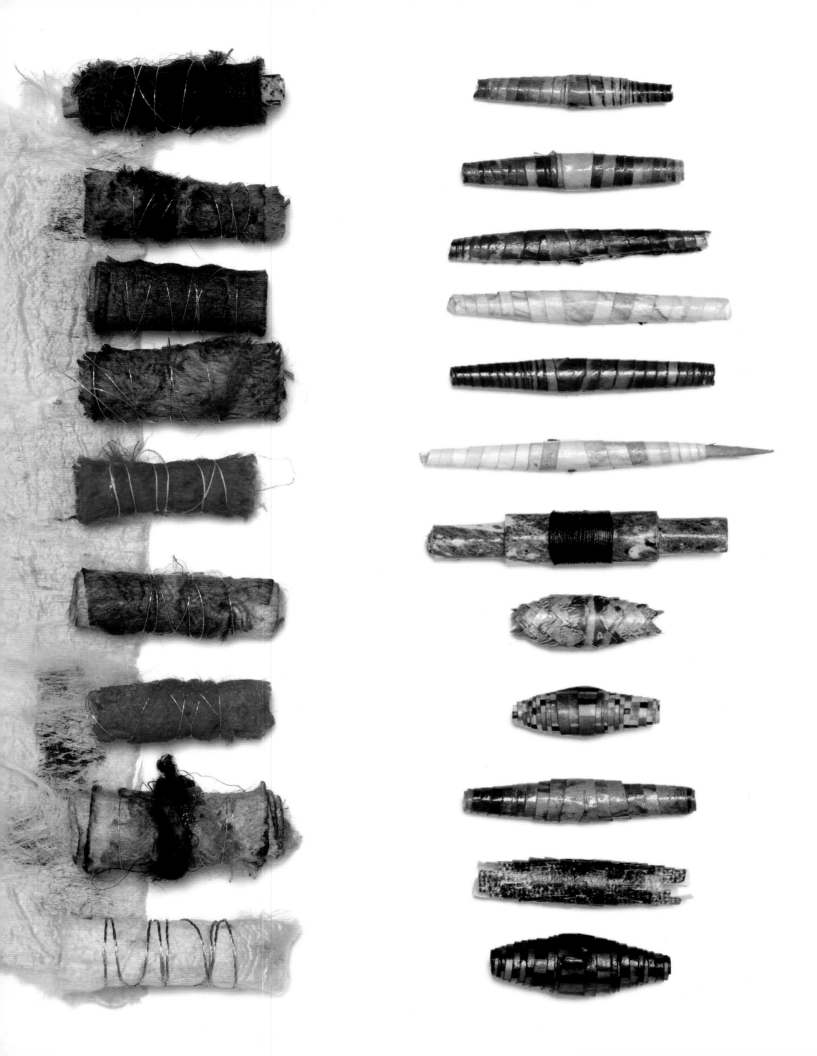

Paper beads look great with the straps. I know you have all made these before and I'm not going to go into the details of making, look on www.d4daisy.com but they do look really super when arranged on a strap. The larger ones could form spacers between stitched motifs for a more formal pattern. Try rolling the carrier rods, too – they make great tags for the ends of cords.

The matchsticks that we used for the spines can also be used for embellishments. Hold them in a cross shape and wrap yarn around the centre. Then wrap around each stick, moving clockwise and going under and over.

Some ideas for decorating the straps.

FAR LEFT: You can see strips of carrier rods, rolled and secured with wrappings of thread.

LEFT: Paper beads are especially good with paper straps. Roll a triangle of decorated paper and secure the end with a blob of glue.

ABOVE and RIGHT: Ideas for using coloured matchsticks.

Using the straps

We've looked at lots of ideas for making the straps – now what can we do with them? You will have seen them popping up in the pics throughout the book, often used as borders or decorative elements. They make a very strong addition to a piece of work – but take care that the colours combine well so that they don't overtake the whole work.

Here are some ideas:

- vessels

- book closures

- bag straps

- wearable art – facings etc.

- exciting surfaces built up on a 'strappy' background

- woven panels.

Some of these are obvious but some are worth examining in greater detail.

This panel is based on the design of a Celtic spear. The background is composed of paper straps, built up from layers of painted and stencilled paper. These include delicate Japanese papers in addition to scraps of the newspaper which were used as table covers when painting.

VESSELS

The straps made from silk pods are particularly suitable for this –
don't strip them down to too many layers if a vessel is planned and
the strap will be good and firm. Wind a long strap around itself – if
this is difficult, use the inside of a kitchen paper roll as a base while it
is pinned. Be inventive: wind up and down, add tight curly rolls at
the start and finish. Stab stitch by hand when the shape is pleasing.
Add motifs, also by hand.

This vessel by Anna Nowicki
is composed of carrier rod
straps, decorated with machine
patterns, which are built up
to form the sides of a vessel.
These were then lashed with
wrapped cords to supporting
dowel rods. The decoration of
paper beads and tassels adds
enormously to the charm of
the piece.

BOOK CLOSURES AND WRAPS

Glue the strap to the back of the book. Make it big enough to wrap around several times for extra impact. A shaped closure could be made – look at the image above. This is also fastened to the back by gluing near the spine.

Val Campbell-Harding introduced me to the idea of straps made from carrier rods. In this book wrap, she built up the straps to form a shape and applied motifs on top.

Weaving

This is an obvious use for straps and makes wonderful cushions. Use firm straps (vary the width to add interest) and anchor them on a felt or Vilene background by stab stitching through the weaving. Consider making a bag by weaving thicker strips and working in the same way as the cushion. Make a slightly narrower version for the strap and add some of the paper beads as a decorative element.

Another fun thing to do would be to use narrow straps and weave on a small hand loom. Consider using wrapped pipe-cleaners as the warp.

I have found this a difficult book to finish as, once I started experimenting, especially with the straps, it could easily have been twice as big. I do hope that you find this too – and will really stretch some of these ideas and invent many more of your own. Layering really works for me and I'm looking forward to seeing some of the work that you produce using these methods.

A most delightful piece composed of narrow straps formed from pintucked fabrics. The colourful sheer fabrics used were layered, pintucked and cut or torn into strips. They were then loosely woven and secured with stitch. *(Janet Crowther)*